6

THE ✠ TIMES

GRADUATE JOB-HUNTING GUIDE

MARK PARKINSON

KOGAN

First published in 2001

Kogan Page Limited
120 Pentonville Road
London N1 9JN
UK

Kogan Page US
22 Broad Street
Milford CT 06460
USA

© Mark Parkinson, 2001   650·14 PAR

British Library Cataloguing in Publication Data

A CIP record for this book is available from the British Library.

ISBN 0 7494 3418 X

Typeset by Jean Cussons Typesetting, Diss, Norfolk
Printed and bound in Great Britain by Clays Ltd, St Ives plc

Contents

Preface   v

1 The graduate jobs market   1
The six employment routes   2
Working for yourself   4
The employment deal   5
A job for life?   6
Graduate career destinations   6
Degrees and jobs   8
European opportunities   11
Fairness in the jobs market   14
Key facts   19

2 Planning your career   21
The six answers   21
Looking forward   23
Deciding what you want to do   24
What you have to offer   33
Putting it all together   50

3 Finding the right job   56
The jobs market   56
Advertised jobs   57
Agencies and executive search   68
Job fairs and networking   70

Weaving a net   71
Cold canvassing   73
Final words   75

4 Applying for jobs   **77**
Application forms   77
The curriculum vitae   89
Etiquette and covering letters   95

5 Assessment procedures   **98**
Psychometric tests   98
Interviews   113
Assessment centres   121
The moment of truth   128

6 Starting work   **130**
Employment contracts   130
Induction and development   133
Appraisals   140
Development centres   143
Staying employed   144
Finale   148

References   **149**
Index   **152**

Preface

Welcome to *The Times Graduate Job-Hunting Guide*. This is designed to help you through the application maze and provide you with practical advice on how to get the job you want.

Most students and new graduates find job-hunting a time-consuming and uncertain process. This book gives you the information you need to cut through the confusion and understand how to find and keep a job. Examples and action points support each section, every one designed to set you on the right path.

The Times Graduate Job-Hunting Guide covers:

- The jobs market and graduate career destinations.
- Deciding what you want to do and what you have to offer.
- How to find jobs and understand advertisements.
- Writing CVs and making sense of application forms.
- Preparing for tests, interviews and assessment centres.
- Understanding the small print of employment contracts.
- What to look for in graduate development programmes.
- Appraisals, development centres and staying employed!

Where appropriate, further reading has been suggested and links have been given to suitable Web sites. Make use of this extra information, as it will add to the power and persuasive quality of your applications. Make no mistake, job hunting is hard work, but if you follow the tips in this book you should be rewarded with a successful start to your career.

The graduate jobs market

The 21st century has seen graduate employment rates hit new heights. Job prospects are good and most graduates find positions that they consider to be satisfactory. Opportunities are broadening as organisations move into new activities and markets, such as e-commerce and cross-border trade. Indeed technology, competition and consumerism are changing the ways in which everyone works. Consequently the labour market, especially in western countries, is increasingly dominated by 'white collar' jobs. Fortunately these are the very jobs for which advanced skills and training are essential. IT, for instance, an increasingly popular sector amongst graduates, offers more and more job opportunities.

Now the bad news! Whatever you may have been led to believe, a degree, even a good degree, is not a meal ticket for life. In 1999, 250,000 people graduated with a first degree. Amazingly this is nearly 10 times as many as 40 years ago; back in those days only 30,000 started first degree courses at the 31 UK universities. The result is that there are a lot more graduates chasing proportionately fewer 'good' jobs. The traditional graduate jobs in management and the professions have not kept pace with the explosion in numbers. Make no mistake, there are still good jobs, but employers can afford to pick the best.

The six employment routes

There is no such thing as a typical graduate job. To put it simply, job diversity has replaced job certainty, with the result that it is now possible to identify six main routes into employment.

Fast-track training schemes

These are still what many people associate with graduate jobs. However, there are comparatively few openings and they tend to be centred on large national or multinational organisations; recruitment into the upper levels of the Civil Service also falls into this category. Competition for places is cut-throat, and strong intellectual and personal skills are essential.

Professional careers

These cover activities such as accountancy, teaching, IT and engineering. There can still be intense competition in some quarters, for example in accountancy, but this is nowhere near as intense as with fast-track schemes. Indeed for some types of engineering and other technical professions there are often more places than applicants.

Administrative jobs

These often include managerial activities but career prospects may be limited. Indeed 'lateral' promotion is now becoming more common, with graduates increasing their skills and experience without necessarily climbing the career ladder. There are many such positions in the retail and financial sectors, where graduates often find themselves working alongside non-graduates and experienced internal candidates.

Small firms

Large recruiters now have to compete against small to medium-sized companies who hire a few graduates each year. Figures suggest that 42 per cent of employed graduates work in businesses employing less than 250 people. This is a trend that is likely to continue with the development of new forms of trading such as e-commerce.

Self-employment

This is the destination of many art and design students and is often the preferred option for those who place lifestyle above financial reward. However, an increasing number of graduates also see the entrepreneurial route as offering the best chance of achieving their ambitions (see 'Working for yourself').

Non-traditional graduate jobs

These are often lower-level jobs where graduates can add significant value to the activity. For instance, it is calculated that almost one-quarter of graduates are secretaries. Of course this includes those who are 'temping' to earn a living; but it also covers those who are engaged in the usual sort of secretarial or personal assistant (PA) type duties.

Finally there is the rest of the jobs market in which being a graduate may not be an advantage. Many enter jobs that require no particular qualifications or earn a living from using specialist skills. There are numerous graduates involved in trade and craft activities, for example in the construction industry, or who run shops, deliver the milk or the post. As with all human endeavours, it is a question of individual choice and interest.

Working for yourself

It is worth spending a little time considering the self-employment option, as this is a form of work that many fail to consider. The sort of graduates who tend to move into self-employment often have better class degrees and are more likely to have work experience. More women than men also seem to be willing to consider such a career, as do those with a family background of self-employment. As has been mentioned, art and design students are often drawn to this form of employment, but it is also becoming an important destination for those with highly saleable technical skills, such as computer and IT graduates. Indeed many are starting businesses while still attending university or college.

Graduates choose self-employment because it offers independence and flexibility. The chance to be your own boss means that you control what you do, and if you employ other people, what they do as well. You decide where to work, what to do, and how much you wish to achieve. Of course this sounds too good to be true and it must be recognised that any failures are also your own, and that if you don't do any work you won't earn any money! That being said, many relish the freedom self-employment provides, especially the fact that it is not a nine-to-five job.

Surveys of graduate self-employment reveal that three in five have no employees or partners and work on their own, although as most are offering services they will have daily contact with clients, customers, suppliers and so forth. The majority work for an average of 40 hours per week, with a significant proportion clocking up 60 hours or more, so self-employment is not an easy option in terms of hours worked. Earning levels are also quite variable, with the median annual salary being £8,000. However this disguises the fact that three-quarters earn £18,000 or more, which as you will see is a salary that compares well with graduates in more traditional forms of employment.

There are many sources of help with starting your own business. If you are drawn to the idea, contact your local Business Link and Enterprise Agency (addresses in the Yellow Pages). Start-up capital and support is offered by organisations such as The Prince's Youth Business Trust, which assists 18–29-year-olds who want to run their own business. The Shell LiveWire outreach programme also offers valuable advice and guidance. Visit the Web site at www.shell-livewire.org. Finally, all the main banks offer free start-up packs and special deals for new businesses.

The employment deal

Across the board, at the time of going to press, the typical graduate starting salary is around £16,500. For blue-chip employers this rises to £17,500 and progresses to £24,000 after three years' service. Consultancy firms offer the highest starting salaries with £19,000 being the average. For comparison the average UK non-graduate wage is £14,500. This puts a premium of between £2,000 and £3,000 on having a degree. It should also be remembered that graduate pay often rises more quickly, in particular in managerial jobs, than for those who do not possess a degree, so by the age of 30–35, male graduates earn about 55 per cent more than male non-graduates, and female graduates 63 per cent more than their contemporaries.

The wise job-hunter will also realise that many of the figures quoted in the media concentrate on the more newsworthy offers, for instance the 'golden hellos', in effect the 'signing-up' fee, offered by some firms (see Chapter 6). It should also be remembered that salaries vary with age, experience and location, quite apart from the fact that they may be performance-related. A sales position can look highly desirable because good performers earn £30,000–£50,000 per year. However, in reality the basic salary is likely to be well below £20,000. Likewise a modest salary may be compensated for by a host of benefits and bonus payments.

A job for life?

So the pay's good, but what about the rest of the deal? As you have seen, there are a number of routes into 'graduate' employment, and by no means all graduates work for large organisations. It is also true that a graduate career does not automatically mean rapid promotion. This has nothing to do with the quality of graduates but is a result of organisations becoming flatter and less hierarchical. Indeed over the last few decades most organisations have been busy removing entire layers of management and encouraging employees to move sideways into different departments or functions. Certainly the job for life is long gone, and in any case most graduates move rapidly between different employers. Many move jobs every two or three years.

The corollary of flatter organisations and job mobility is that graduates need continually to develop their skills and talents, not only to perform their present job, but also to make themselves more attractive to future employers. This really is the age of 'lifelong learning' and if you think that your degree marks the end of the educational process, think again. Your degree is only the start.

Graduate career destinations

A quick look at the latest graduate data shows that 66 per cent of graduates go straight into employment. A further 8 per cent start studying for a higher degree, and 9 per cent go into some other form of further study or training. Of the remainder some move overseas or take up voluntary work, and only 6 per cent classify themselves as unemployed.

Turning our attention to the sort of work that graduates do, the major areas of employment are broken down as follows:

Clerical and secretarial occupations	13%
Commercial, industrial and public sector managers	12%
Teaching professionals	8%
Other professional occupations (eg law)	8%
Information technology professionals	7%
Retail and catering occupations	6%
Health professionals	5%
Business and finance (eg: accountancy)	5%
Engineering professionals	5%
Media, literary and design professionals	5%
Marketing, sales, PR and advertising	4%
Scientific research (eg: physicists)	2%

(*Source*: UCAS, 2000)

Another way of exploring the data is to look at employment rates for particular degree subjects. So in terms of the highest employment rates the top 12 subjects are:

Veterinary science	95%
Medicine and dentistry	91%
Computer science	84%
Accountancy	83%
Business and management studies	80%
Civil engineering	78%
Electrical and electronic engineering	77%
Mechanical engineering	77%
Media studies	77%
Building	74%
Drama	73%
Economics	71%

(*Source*: THES, 1999)

The highest employment rates are in subjects related to medicine because there are a limited number of graduates and a high demand. Technical graduates such as engineers, computer scientists and IT professionals are also prized because the number of jobs outstrips the number of suitably qualified candidates. However, it is interesting to note that high rates of employment for particular subjects do not automatically imply low rates of unemployment. For example a subject such as law has a very low unemployment and employment rate! This is because of the large numbers who go on to do further study. This is often also the case for graduates in subjects like drama or media, who in addition often gain employment in lower-level jobs or those that are not related to their degree discipline.

On the question of degree discipline, although some jobs obviously require graduates with particular qualifications, employers will often consider those with degrees in any subject. In total about a third of all graduate jobs are open to those with degrees in 'any discipline'. That is because the right skills and experience are often more important than the knowledge accumulated as part of a degree.

Degrees and jobs

There are well over 100 single honours degree subjects, but most fall into six core areas. The following provides details on typical career and job destinations for those holding particular degrees.

Arts, creative arts and humanities

This degree area covers English, history, modern languages, drama, design and media studies. Interestingly about one-third of graduates in these areas gain positions in firms employing fewer than 50 people. This is perhaps a reflection of the 'creative' content of some of these subjects, and that creative businesses are often small to medium-sized enterprises. That being said, the essentially non-vocational nature of arts degrees means that graduates enter the full range of generalist 'graduate' jobs. Those with language skills are always in high demand, a fact illustrated by the 50 per cent or so who go on to gain employment through paid work experience.

Business and administrative studies

The number of business graduates entering employment is higher than the average for all other degree disciplines. Perhaps this is no surprise as business studies includes subjects such as accountancy, and well over half of the graduates in accountancy enter the business and finance professions. In fact the majority, 9 out of 10, go into chartered, certified or management accountancy positions. Of the graduates in the more general business subjects, about a quarter secure positions in commercial or public sector management posts. As with many other graduates, many of the remainder start their careers in clerical or secretarial posts.

Engineering and building management

The construction and engineering industries are strongly influenced by the health of the economy. At present with a relatively strong economy there is a need for all types of engineer. However, competition for places is intense and the overall number in the engineering and building professions is not expected to increase markedly over the next few years. That being said, most types of engineer are more likely to find immediate employment than the average graduate. Most of these go into engineering jobs but there is also a significant percentage who move into business and management positions. Of all the engineering disciplines, electronic engineers are in particular demand, especially in the aerospace industry. The outlook for building professionals is a little patchier, but there is still a good demand. Most graduates continue to study for professional qualifications, and of course subjects such as architecture demand significant additional practical and academic study on top of a first degree.

Mathematical sciences and IT

It is fair to say that there is not a typical destination for graduates in these disciplines, as the skills developed are in great demand across all industrial sectors. However, a large number enter the computing industry and work in specialist firms of all sizes. IT and software engineering firms in particular are often small businesses that employ a limited number of highly qualified individuals, but deal with clients on a global basis. Over the last 5 to 10 years the Internet has also become a key element in the way in which such firms work. Pure mathematicians may find work in specialist areas and, for example, may study to become accountants or actuaries. However, many stay within the educational system and study for higher degrees.

Science

Graduates in the core sciences such as biology, chemistry and physics are well equipped to enter both scientific and non-scientific jobs. Analytic skills, numerical ability and IT familiarity make science graduates particularly attractive to employers. Science teachers are also in demand and there are a number of schemes designed to attract science graduates into the teaching profession. About half the graduates in chemistry and physics go into scientific or technical jobs, and in the case of physics half of these are in IT. In contrast about a third of biologists and environmental scientists move into scientific jobs, with a much higher proportion starting off in clerical or secretarial work. Of the professional 'medical' graduates, virtually all go straight into employment related to their degree.

Social sciences

While the number of social science graduates immediately entering employment is lower than for graduates as a whole, those that do enter employment go into a broad range of different jobs. Economics, law and geography graduates seem to be particularly successful in entering the business and finance sectors, whereas psychology and sociology graduates often move into managerial positions. In the case of psychology, many continue their studies and work towards becoming chartered psychologists. As there are no vocational social science first degrees, more social science graduates continue with postgraduate studies than for any other discipline.

If you would like more information on the career destinations of UK graduates, the Universities and Colleges Admissions Service (UCAS) publishes a range of useful information. Look out for What Do Graduates Do?, which is published each year. The Times Higher Education Supplement (THES) also conducts regular surveys.

European opportunities

The onward march of the multinational business means that there are many more opportunities in Europe and the rest of the world. The major companies need to recruit the best graduates, wherever they come from, if they are to be successful at a global level. In a similar way graduates will increasingly require an international outlook and need to be prepared to work in a number of different countries.

Across Europe the major sectors of work are retailing, IT, telecommunications, financial services and manufacturing. The retail industry is particularly large and employs over 15 million people in 4 million enterprises. Naturally many of these businesses are small, but the big ones are very big indeed. Germany, for example, has five retail organisations in the world top 10. Many retailers are establishing a presence outside their home market, and there is often a movement of managerial personnel between countries. Over recent years a number of foreign retailers have moved into the UK, from the supermarket group Aldi to the home products chain Ikea. Needless to say the traffic is not just one-way: the UK's own Kingfisher group, which includes Woolworths, B&Q, Comet and Superdrug, also owns the European retailers Darty and Castorama. The group employs 125,000 people in 14 different countries and makes 40 per cent of its sales outside the UK. The point is that these are businesses that span countries, and the opportunities for graduates flow from their truly international basis.

Major growth areas in IT include networking, consultancy and training, e-commerce, multimedia, Internet and intranet, to name but a few. The sector has grown hugely over the last few years as developments in IT are driving business growth in other sectors. The employers of graduates are usually the larger European or North American manufacturers, such as Nortel. There are also many opportunities with software companies and consultancies. For those who are interested in jobs in this area, or telecommunications, the important thing is to join an international organisation. The other thing to remember is that you do not need a specialist IT, electronics or engineering degree for many of the jobs.

The financial services sector is also going through a period of rapid expansion. Factors such as deregulation, new technology, the single European market and the Euro all mean that most large financial organisations are restructuring and reorganising on an unprecedented scale. The traditional banks are changing, as are insurance firms and those offering support services such as accountancy. Indeed all the major players are now global businesses. The big American firms such as Merrill Lynch and Goldman Sachs operate in most European countries, and have large bases in London and Frankfurt; and Anglo-German businesses like Dresdner Kleinwort Benson also have numerous European offices. All this means that there is a strong demand for graduates wishing to work in the international money markets.

At a European level manufacturing is still an important employer, employing almost a quarter of the workforce. As with the other sectors there is an increasing trend for organisations to work in cross-border partnerships and for the workforce to be spread across a number of different countries. Indeed some high technology engineering projects can now only be achieved on a pan-European basis. Think no further than Airbus Industries or British Aerospace. The latter is a partner in 29 major international projects, is Britain's largest manufacturing exporter, and Europe's principal aerospace and defence company. Firms like British Aerospace, and the other major manufacturers, recruit management and technical staff from all countries.

The upshot is that there is strong demand in the retail, IT, telecommunications and manufacturing sectors. There is also scope in less obvious areas such as law and management consultancy. International law is a small but growing area of legal work. EU legislation allows for multinational partnerships, and the amount of cross-border work is increasing accordingly. Consequently an international legal career has become a viable option for those interested in combining the legal disciplines of a number of different countries.

Management consultants help organisations with a wide range of business problems. For example, McKinsey & Company is a professional consultancy firm that advises senior management on issues such as strategy, organisational change, operations and IT. McKinsey has 78 offices in all the major business centres in Europe and across the world. They work with businesses of all sizes and recruit graduates from any discipline. Management consultancy is a popular choice for those seeking an international career, but it is essential to join the right sort of firm. The big players are organisations such as

McKinsey and the Boston Consulting Group; and those linked to accountancy firms such as KPMG and Price-WaterhouseCoopers.

There are also many opportunities to work within the government of the European Union and its associated bodies. However, whether the employer is in the governmental or private sectors, most will expect applicants to have some language skills. Apart from English, German or French are often required.

Fairness in the jobs market

In many ways the graduate jobs market is very traditional, and while taking a degree boosts employment prospects, certain groups still experience difficulties in securing a good 'graduate' job. In this section we look at whether going to a particular university makes a difference in the job hunt, and also the particular problems encountered by mature and female graduates.

The right university

As you would expect, graduates are usually asked about their qualifications and work experience at interview. However, many employers also pay particular attention to the university or college attended. In fact about two-thirds of major employers, such as the supermarket group Asda, target a relatively small number of named institutions. In the case of Asda these include the universities of Leeds, Manchester, Bristol and Newcastle.

Employers pick particular universities on the basis of tradition and reputation, in particular those with high entry requirements. They are also influenced by their past experiences with particular institutions, especially if a certain university has supplied good quality graduates in previous years. Naturally it is also a question of money! It is a good deal cheaper to concentrate on a few places, rather than cover the entire higher education sector. Another fact worth mentioning is that employers seem to discriminate against graduates from the 'new' universities. At least this is the message that emerges from a recent survey by the graduate recruitment specialists, Park Human Resources. They found that 85 per cent of employers believed that the new universities produced graduates of a lower quality than the older institutions, despite other research which suggests that the new universities produce graduates who are more business orientated, and of equal intellectual ability.

The consequence of selection at a university level is that some institutions boast much higher employment rates for their graduates than others. For example, over 80 per cent of those who graduate from Aston University find employment within six months. However, there are some big provisos on headline figures such as these. The statistics do not discriminate between different types of jobs and include everything from management trainees to those working as secretaries. Also, especially with a university like Aston, little is done to distinguish between those places that predominantly host vocational courses and those that are more 'academic'. Aston happens to specialise in subjects such as business, engineering, pharmacy and optometry.

Does this mean that you are disadvantaged if you have been to the 'wrong' university? At one level the answer is 'yes'. You will find it harder to get a job with a major employer if you have attended an institution that is not on their list. At another level your prospects are brighter, because most graduates do not work for large organisations. The bulk of jobs are with small to medium-sized companies, and of course, large government-related organisations and services. In this way you are no worse off than any other graduate: your degree and university matter, but so do your experience, abilities and personality.

Mature graduates

The sort of person who graduates from a university or college has changed markedly over the years. The 21-year-old white middle-class student, with a good degree from a recognised university, accounts for only a small percentage of those who graduate.

There are now far more graduates from all social classes, ethnic minorities, and of course, an enormous increase in those who choose to enter higher education later in life. Presently over a quarter of those graduating are over the age of 30. However, a poll of the UK's top companies reveals that only 4 per cent of last year's recruits were mature graduates. Unfortunately the older you are, the poorer your chances of getting a job with any of the country's blue-chip companies. There are but a few honourable exceptions. For example, the computer manufacturer Hewlett-Packard operates a 'diversity' policy and encourages older graduates, women, ethnic minorities and the disabled to apply for its graduate development programmes.

On the face of it this is rather gloomy news. It is also perplexing given that mature graduates often have knowledge, skills and experience that their younger colleagues could not possibly possess. Does it amount to deliberate discrimination by employers? Not necessarily, as employers claim that they receive few applications for graduate training schemes from mature candidates. However this is a poor defence and it is an unfortunate truth that the employment practices of many large organisations leave much to be desired.

On the positive side there are moves to combat age discrimination. There has also been a significant shift in the proportion of graduates recruited by large organisations. Ten years ago 100 of the largest employers took 80 per cent of graduates, whereas now they only recruit about 10 per cent. What this means is that graduates, whatever their age, cannot rely on getting a job with a major employer. Everyone must cast their net wider and consider all the available options.

Female graduates

There are fewer female than male applicants to companies in the science, engineering and technology (SET) sectors. The reasons are numerous, but women are more likely to study the arts or social sciences, and despite initiatives by SET organisations to recruit more female graduates, those women with appropriate degrees are still more likely to enter other areas. Even more worrying, employers in sectors such as finance and banking are also starting to favour SET graduates because of their numerical skills. What this amounts to is that women's chances of getting jobs in a large part of the economy are severely reduced.

However, prospects are better for those who have decided to enter general management or to become lawyers or accountants. Women seem to do just as well as men when it comes to getting onto management trainee programmes or into the professions. To take law as an example, the Law Society reports that there has been an increase of over 150 per cent in women practising law in the last 10 years. Indeed 51 per cent of new entrants and 34 per cent of practising solicitors are now female. In addition, in 1998 Heather Hallet became the first female chair of the Bar Council.

However, even in the professions women often have a struggle to rise to the same level as men. After five years or so men have often secured more promotion than their female colleagues. In many ways this reflects the underlying unfairness of many promotion procedures and the effects of the masculine culture and attitudes that prevail in many organisations. Numerous surveys attest to the fact that there are still plenty of obstacles in the way of the professional woman. In particular these factors have an impact:

- the 'old school tie' network;
- people, usually men, staying in top jobs for a long time;

- ▓ less mentoring or support for women;
- ▓ office politics (and the fact that women do not wish to play);
- ▓ women assuming that competence and ability are enough;
- ▓ family responsibilities.

To take just one of these factors, men often interact with senior managers (potential mentors) in a sporting or social context. They therefore have plenty of opportunity to build up personal relationships outside the workplace. Corporate entertainment may also involve taking clients to events such as football or rugby matches. Women are far less likely to meet their mentors, or clients, under such circumstances.

Yet despite issues such as these, there is one thing that will change the outlook for women permanently: demographics. Before too long women will make up 65 per cent of all new employees, and more than half of the workplace. It is anticipated that women will secure over 60 per cent of all higher-level jobs by 2005. So while female graduates may have some difficulties in the short term, the situation is changing. After all, in the last decade a number of women have moved into a number of high profile 'masculine' jobs. These include positions such as airline captains, the head of MI5 and the speaker of the House of Commons.

Ethnic minorities

Many employers recognise the benefits of having a diverse workforce, but unfair employment practices still exist. However, with greater numbers of ethnic minority graduates, and a need to fill an increasing number of graduate jobs, the opportunities are there. Indeed a commitment to recruiting the best, and to achieving a balanced workforce, is often one and the same thing. That is not to say that ethnic minority graduates do not still encounter difficulties. There have been many well-publicised cases, but help is at hand. There are a number of positive action schemes that offer insights into particular occupations and career development support. These include the Windsor Fellowship, Midland Bank's Fellowship and a number of others. You can access information on support groups and recruitment issues through specialist Web sites such as www.kaleidoscopic.co.uk.

While many claim that the issue of discrimination is overblown, people still seem to miss out on opportunities, or worse still, experience actual harassment. It is also a fact that the unemployment rate among ethnic minority groups is more than twice that for white people. If you feel that you have been actively discriminated against, contact the Commission for Racial Equality (CRE). The CRE Head Office is at Elliot House, 10-12 Allington Street, London SW1E 5EH. Telephone: 020 7828 7022.

Key facts

- In 1999, 250,000 people graduated with a first degree.
- Graduate unemployment, at 6 per cent, is currently at a 10-year low.
- About 30 per cent of graduates have a job offer before leaving university.
- Some employers favour graduates from particular universities, especially the older 'traditional' institutions.
- Not all graduates work for large blue-chip organisations. It is estimated that 900,000 work in firms employing less than 250 people.
- The areas of the economy experiencing the greatest growth are sales, customer service, engineering and IT.
- Overall, graduates in medical and health sciences,

business, education, computer science, engineering and technology are most in demand.

■ One in nine graduates work in IT or engineering-related jobs.

■ Twenty-five per cent of graduates go on to postgraduate studies.

■ The average graduate starting salary is £17,400. After one year it rises to £19,500, and after three to £24,000. (The average UK non-graduate wage is £14,500.)

■ Nearly 25 per cent of employers offer incentives to graduates, such as joining bonuses.

■ Most 'new' graduates change jobs every two to three years.

2

Planning your career

You are likely to spend up to one-third of your life at work. For most people this will amount to at least 50,000 hours, so it is important that you find a job (and a career) you enjoy. From the employers' perspective it is also essential that you do your job competently. This chapter is about identifying the sort of job you would like and, of course, what you can offer an employer.

The six answers

In order to find a job you will enjoy, you need to have a good idea of what it will be like. The better your idea, the easier it will be to find. You should also recognise that you need to open your mind to all possibilities, rather than exclude options because of faulty assumptions or even fear. In fact if you consider the question, 'What do you want to do?' there are six types of answer:

▪ **'I can't do what I want to do.'** It is actually quite hard work to pretend that you could do anything. It confronts head-on an internal dialogue many of us have had since childhood, often expressed as: 'Don't wish too much for something, you might not get it.' This is closely followed by, 'It wouldn't have been that good anyway.' However, at this stage of career planning it is important to suspend your doubts and to imagine what you would like to do, if you could do anything.

■ **'It doesn't matter what I want to do.'** This is another rather pessimistic approach and rests on the assumption that what you want is not important. What you want is very important! Don't put yourself down, clear away your doubts, and acknowledge that you deserve a satisfying job just as much as anybody else.

■ **'I already know what I want to do.'** There is nothing wrong with knowing what you want, but remember that jobs and careers evolve. You might find it useful to explore your wishes and wants in more detail. The results are likely to be surprising and could change what you considered to be settled.

■ **'I am afraid of what I want to do.'** Our wishes often seem unattainable, impossible, bound to lead to disappointment, failure, embarrassment or even ridicule. Yet we all know that our greatest satisfaction often comes from confronting our fears and doing things that we initially thought were impossible. Time to think the unthinkable!

■ **'I don't know what I want to do.'** Some people seem to have known since birth that they want to be a doctor, a lawyer, a teacher, an artist, an engineer or whatever. Others (perhaps the majority) do not have a strong sense of vocation. If you are one of the latter, now is the time to discover your interests, preferences, values and motivations.

■ **'I know what I want, but it doesn't involve work.'** This is an interesting starting point, but on the face of it rather impractical. Alas, unless you have private wealth, you are unlikely to be able to take this route. Perhaps the compromise is to create your own job and work for yourself. This is an option that still requires you to do some serious thinking about what it is that you want.

Looking forward

Whichever of the 'six answers' seems to fit your current frame of mind, you may find it useful to clarify your thoughts using a simple exercise. This 'personal vision' technique can help to set the scene for what comes next.

Imagine that you have achieved your dreams. What would your life be like? How do you think you would feel? How would you describe yourself? More specifically:

■ **Life purpose.** Project yourself into the future and try to decide what 'big' things you would like to achieve in life. What are your aspirations? For yourself? For others? For society?

■ **Self-image.** If you could be exactly the sort of person you wanted to be, what would you be like? Describe your 'ideal' personality. What would you be good at? What skills would you have?

■ **Work.** If you could do anything, what would be your ideal job, profession or vocation? What would you like to achieve through work?

■ **Relationships.** What type and quality of relationships would you like to have with a partner, your family, your friends, or at work?

■ **Home.** Where do you see yourself living? What's it like? How can you achieve your dream?

■ **Personal achievement.** What have you achieved outside work? What new things have you learnt?

Make a note of your thoughts and work carefully through the rest of the chapter. When you have finished, come back to your 'personal vision' and see how the other things you have learnt complement (or change) your ideas.

Deciding what you want to do

This section looks at the three main job 'wants', namely, what aspects of work engage your interest, what personal values you have and how they relate to work, and what motivates you to do a good job.

Interests

It probably goes without saying that interests go hand in hand with job satisfaction. You will get far more satisfaction, enjoyment and sense of fulfilment if you do a job you like. However, how do you decide what interests you? It is obviously physically impossible to research every job, although there are many good books that provide details on the major career areas. Try looking through the careers advisers' standard reference book, *Occupations*, published by the Careers and Occupational Information Centre (COIC). This is updated each year and contains information on over 600 jobs and careers. Obviously there are more than 600 different types of job, but did you know that 90 per cent of the population are spread between 300 jobs, and 50 per cent are in just 50? The latter includes jobs such as teaching.

Fortunately there are some fundamental ways in which jobs differ from each other. One of the most obvious distinctions is between jobs that predominantly concern people or information or things:

■ **People jobs.** If you are a 'people person' you will be drawn to jobs involving helping, caring, advising and persuading. In a helping situation you might be teaching or training somebody to do something by guiding, tutoring and communicating facts and ideas. If you are caring you will have assumed a more 'hands-on' role and may well be treating, healing or nursing other people. The advising person is providing specific help and advice to other people, but usually not in a hands-on way: so, for example, you might be providing legal or financial advice. In contrast the persuading individual will be actively influencing other people, and probably trying to sell them products or services. Many managerial jobs contain a large persuasive element.

Examples: teacher, trainer, health professional, therapist, social worker, community worker, travel agent, sales person, public relations, management.

Questions: What sort of people person do you think you are? Are you a mixture of two or more of the different people types? Do you prefer to work in one-to-one situations, groups or teams, or are you more interested in working directly with the public?

■ **Information jobs.** These involve dealing with data, facts and figures and quantities. People are attracted to these sorts of jobs because they can gather, analyse and interpret different sorts of information. Those who gather and organise information are concerned with detail and like compiling, searching and researching. Many administrative jobs require these sorts of qualities. The Analyst wants to know what it means, and will take data and transform it in some way, maybe by subjecting it to a statistical or financial analysis. Finally the interpreter wants to know how to apply the fruits of analysis to decision making and planning.

Examples: Civil Servant, accountant, economist, banker, auditor, marketing executive, quantity surveyor, systems analyst, researcher.

Questions: Most jobs have a data dimension, but are you attracted to careers that involve a lot of number-crunching? If so, what sort? Are you a researcher or are you more interested in applying what you have discovered?

▓ **Thing jobs.** The word 'thing' implies working with inanimate objects, but within this area are included all types of agricultural and environmental work. However, there is a division between directly practical jobs and those that are technical or scientific. The practical dimension includes creating, making, modelling, constructing, manufacturing and maintaining things. All are activities that often require good manual dexterity and an eye for detail. Technical jobs involve the application of particular scientific, mechanical, electrical, electronic or similar principles. They may also require the use of the hands but technical knowledge is often more important. Finally scientific jobs require extensive specialist knowledge and professional expertise.

Examples: architect, builder, engineer, physicist, pharmacist, pathologist, geologist, biotechnologist, veterinary surgeon.

Questions: Do you like to work with your hands? Are you interested in how things work? Do you enjoy conducting experiments? Do you have a scientific approach to solving problems?

You also need to think about any creative interests you might possess. These can be applied to the people–information–things distinction, and might reinforce jobs in these particular areas, for instance:

- creative (writing) + people = journalist, public relations, publishing;
- creative (technical) + information = software designer, Web developer, astrophysics;
- creative (visual) + things (practical) = fashion designer, graphic artist, photographer.

Where appropriate, other interests such as music or sport will need to be taken into account. To complete the picture, the work environment needs to be added to the equation. Where, in a geographical sense, would you like to work? Are you prepared to move to a different part of the country or even to a different country? What sort of climate suits you? And what about the working conditions? Do you want to be inside or outside? Work in an office, on-site or in 'the field'? In a laboratory, production facility or a factory? And so on.

Action steps

- Assess your interests using the descriptions provided. Do you have one major area of interest? Why is it more important than the rest? Is it because you have skills in this area and not in the others? If so, would you be interested in the other things if you thought you could do them? (People are trained to do jobs!)
- Do you have a definite rank order ('pecking order') of interests? How do your interests combine with each other? What does this tell you about suitable jobs? Try to pick five jobs that you think fit the bill.
- Do you seem to be equally attracted (or uninterested) in all the main interest areas? Try the exercise again. If all else fails exclude those things you definitely don't like and see what's left. What do they have in common?

Values

By this stage you should have a better idea of what you would be interested in doing. But you might also be hearing a small voice in your head that's saying, 'That's just not me'. The reason for the warning is that some of the jobs you have identified clash with your values system. Values can be described as deeply-held views, even beliefs; certainly they are things that we consider to be important at a moral level. In the work arena certain jobs, and often organisations themselves, have their own value systems. If you are to be comfortable in a job, or working for a big-name company, you need to make sure that your values are the same. Some example values are:

- **Honesty.** Are you going to be able to be open about what you do? Will there be constraints on your freedom of speech? Is the job on the borderline of what society considers to be acceptable?
  Related values: privacy, power and authority.
- **Respect.** Are people treated with respect? Do profits rely on a section of society being exploited? Is there any sense of equality between employee and employer? Where does the power lie?
  Related values: recognition, security.
- **Democracy.** How are decisions made? Are working conditions prescribed or is there room for debate? Do employees have any say in the direction of the organisation? Is there any form of representation?
  Related values: involvement, harmony.
- **Accountability.** Is there some ultimate form of accountability or mechanism for keeping things in check? Is the work governed by codes of conduct, 'watchdog' organisations or professional bodies?
  Related values: order, quality.
- **Ethics.** Is the nature of the job open to attack on ethical grounds? For example, does it concern things

like armaments, nuclear power or biotechnology? Does it cut across religious or cultural divides?
Related values: reputation, integrity.

▧ **Altruism.** Does the job allow individuals to put something back into society or is it merely concerned with profits? Are employees allowed to develop their talents for the good of all? Is cooperative working encouraged?
Related values: public service, community.

Values are coded into our brains at both a conscious and an unconscious level. Sometimes it is not easy to identify what we consider to be important, especially if there is a conflict between our values and other aspects of potential jobs such as money and status. Despite these difficulties, wise job hunters take time to explore their value systems and try to find jobs that fit their views of what is acceptable.

Action steps

▧ Eighteen different values have been mentioned. Imagine that you can only have five. Which are they? Now, imagine that you can only have two. What have you got left? Now only one. What is the most important value?

▧ What would a job (or organisation) be like that had this as a central value? Do such jobs or organisations actually exist? What do you know about them?

▧ Are you setting an impossible requirement? Are you really willing to choose a job, or an organisation, in which your main value (or more realistically, your five main values) are paramount?

Motivation

Motivation and values are related, and the preferences we have as a result of our value systems are often important sources of motivation. However, in simple terms motivation is the energy that we bring to our work. From a personal perspective it is valuable to know what we find energising, and also what tends to turn our energy off. Some sources of motivation are:

- **Pressure.** Some people thrive in pressured working environments and like to have plenty (even too much) to do. Others find it stressful, like to work on a small number of projects at any given time, and need peace to think.
- **Power.** Being 'the boss' or in charge of people, money and resources can be highly motivating. However, some people find it lonely at the top, do not seek responsibility or authority, and are happier following orders rather than issuing them.
- **Achievement.** Some people enjoy work because it provides them with a sense of achievement and personal identity, and provides a means of meeting personal targets and goals. Other people derive their sense of achievement from non-work activities.
- **Competition.** Work provides a great opportunity to compete, so if you are a natural competitor there is plenty of scope to compare your performance with your colleagues. However, there are different sorts of competition, and some are motivated by doing the best they can do, rather than by directly competing with others.
- **Comradeship.** Psychologists call this 'affiliation', and it is the sense of satisfaction to be gained from working as part of a team, or if you like it is the social aspect of work. But not everyone is interested in being part of a team.
- **Recognition.** For many, work is the way in which they gain recognition, praise and acknowledgement from other people. Their job and the status it gives them as

a person are important to them. However, many don't care about recognition, or as with achievement, feel recognised in other ways.

■ **Growth.** People often use work as a way of developing themselves or of learning to do new things. Indeed in enlightened organisations personal development is often seen as an important way of keeping employees content. Then again, it depends in what way you wish to grow: through your career or in a more individualistic way.

■ **Reward.** Money is of course a great motivator. If you are commercially driven with an interest in working in a profit-oriented environment, then business is the place for you. However, bear in mind that other factors may be of equal (or even greater) importance: job security, for example.

■ **Security.** There is no such thing as a totally secure job, but some are more stable and dependable than others. The issue is the value you place on security compared with the other factors you consider important such as growth, status and reward. That being said, most graduates only stay for a relatively short period of time in their first couple of jobs, so security may not be a major concern.

■ **Structure.** Entire books are dedicated to organisational structure, and there is everything from the (almost) completely unstructured, 'flat' organisation to the large bureaucratic multi-division corporation. However, it is important to realise that structure, which younger people often consider to be 'old fashioned', is usually related to predictability and order.

■ **Prestige.** Many people feel happier and are more motivated if they work for a 'big-name' organisation, especially if it is one that espouses the same sort of values as they do. They respect the organisation and feel that the respect in which it is held will reflect well on them.

Bear in mind that prestige, by definition, is generally linked to well-established (and often larger) organisations.

▓ **Progression.** This is about a sense of getting somewhere or of climbing the ladder of promotion. It is a close cousin of motivators such as status and power, and often provides personal impetus to people's careers. As with prestige, elaborate hierarchies, and with them promotion prospects, are more likely to be found in larger organisations.

▓ **Autonomy.** Having a degree of independence and control over one's work activities can be a prime source of motivation. Many people are stimulated by having a freedom of action, and indeed independence is often considered to be both a value and a motivator.

▓ **Drive.** In a work sense drive concerns the motivation that comes from work itself. In many there is a deep social and cultural ethic that leads us to believe that it is our duty to work; beloved of sociologists this is often called the 'Protestant work ethic'.

▓ **Interest.** The range of activities available through work, the opportunities to be creative, and in some jobs to take risks, provide interest and excitement, not least because people usually have access to much better resources at work than they do at home.

Understanding what motivates you can help you decide on the sort of organisational culture that would suit you. For example, if you want plenty of structure, prestige and clear paths of progression, you are probably going to be attracted to large organisations. If things like autonomy and affiliation are important then you may be more in tune with the way in which smaller organisations operate.

Action steps

▓ Imagine that you are writing a job advertisement. Which of the motivation words mentioned would you use to attract attention? Are these the same words that would make you want to read further?

▓ Would different things motivate you if you were considering a long-term commitment to an organisation? Why do you think there is a difference between long-term and short-term sources of motivation? Do you think it is important?

▓ Think very carefully and pick your top five sources of motivation. Now put them in order of priority. These are your career drivers.

What you have to offer

Let us assume that you have, or are expecting, a good degree. You are personable, well spoken and know what sort of jobs interest you. All in all you are likely to make a good first impression and to perform reasonably well in the initial stages of an interview. What's missing? In truth something very important is missing, and that is that you will also have to demonstrate that you have the right abilities, transferable skills, personality and 'work' experience. To impress a potential employer you will need to convince him that you can make an early and positive contribution to the job in question.

Abilities

There are three core abilities that have been shown to be particularly important for graduate level jobs. These are:

▓ **Abstract reasoning.** This is the ability to solve problems from first principles, and in particular to be able to understand the logic that underpins arguments presented in a diagrammatic or symbolic way.

■ **Verbal reasoning.** This is the ability to understand and interpret written information. In a work context this would involve the ability to comprehend closely argued reports and to understand complex written information.

■ **Numerical reasoning.** This is the ability to understand and interpret numerical information. In a work situation this would typically involve the intelligent manipulation of data in tables and charts.

In addition there are a number of other abilities that are more or less important depending on the job. These include spatial and mechanical ability, and speed and accuracy. Spatial ability is the ability to understand how shapes are moved in three-dimensional space and how things fit together; mechanical ability how simple 'machines' work, and the implications of common physical and mechanical principles. Both spatial and mechanical ability are practical in nature, so they often relate to jobs with practical, scientific or design elements. Speed and accuracy are about how quickly detailed information can be checked for inaccuracies, and so these are abilities that are important in any job requiring detail consciousness.

Patterns of ability

More details on abilities are provided in Chapter 5, as they are often measured using psychometric tests. You will also find some example questions so that you will know what to expect if you are assessed in this way. However, it is useful to find out where your strengths lie before applying for jobs, and to appreciate that the pattern of your abilities can provide clues about the jobs that would suit you the best.

While all the three main abilities are useful for most careers, the key ability will vary depending on the job. For example, good abstract or diagrammatic reasoning is essential in many technological jobs such as software engineering and systems programming, quite apart from any job that involves planning. In a similar way verbal ability is the prime requirement in all aspects of administration and management, teaching, law, journalism and broadcasting. And perhaps predictably numerical ability comes to the fore in things like accountancy, banking, marketing and all commercial activities.

The combination of abilities with each other is also characteristic of particular careers. As an example, medicine is often associated with stronger diagrammatic and verbal ability than numerical, whereas engineers often have strong numerical and diagrammatic ability coupled to a lower level of verbal capability.

Action steps

■ Think about the six main abilities mentioned and put them in rank order, starting with the strongest. What does this tell you about what you can offer an employer? What does it say about the sort of jobs that might suit you?

■ If you have difficulty putting your abilities in order you might like to consider visiting your university or college careers service. They will be able to provide you with tests that you can use to assess your abilities.

■ If you have access to the Internet you can visit the SHL Student Direct Web site where timed tests are available. The address is www.shlgroup.com/direct.

Transferable skills

These days employers demand graduates with 'transferable' skills. These are the skills that enhance personal effectiveness and so make people better at the jobs they do. They also happen to be the skills employers are talking about when they say that they want 'well-rounded' individuals; and unfortunately it is those that they say are often lacking in graduate job applicants.

A number of surveys have shown that among the most sought after skills are:

- team working;
- commitment;
- communication;
- flexibility;
- customer orientation;
- business awareness;
- problem solving;
- organisation;
- numeracy.

You will probably notice that this is a somewhat jumbled list and that, for instance, numeracy has already been mentioned under abilities. However, as you will see, transferable skills do actually fall into four main groups; and numerical aptitude and numerical application is not necessarily the same thing!

Over the next few pages we will look carefully at a fuller list of skills because you must connect your educational experience, and work experience if you have any, with the appropriate transferable skills. This knowledge will make a considerable difference to the success of your job applications and interview performance.

People skills

People or interpersonal skills include teamworking, spoken communication, persuading (influencing) skills, networking, dealing with conflict and understanding other people's points of view (sensitivity).

Teamworking

This is all about working effectively with other people towards some particular goal. In practice it involves collecting, sharing and using information, supporting and challenging people, building on other people's ideas or actions, consensus decision making and being able to put personal ambition aside for the good of the team.

▨ Make a list of all the groups or teams (work, academic, research, sports, social) you have been involved with, now or in the recent past. What was your role? How much time and effort did you put in? What did you do to help set up or organise the group?

Spoken communication

Virtually any graduate job you care to mention will involve considerable communication with colleagues, subordinates, managers, suppliers, clients or customers. You will need to be able to communicate your thoughts in a clear and unambiguous way at the correct level (register) for your particular audience.

▨ Think about the times you have given a talk or a presentation to a group. How did you decide what to say? How did you manage things like timing? How did you keep people interested? How was your talk received?

Influencing

This concerns being able to influence the opinions and attitudes of other people, to negotiate and bring others to the point of agreement. Influencing skills are at the centre of all forms of negotiation and selling activity. Indeed if you know a good salesperson you would find it useful to sit in on a sales meeting. Take particular note of how to gain the trust of another person and to develop a rapport.

▨ Identify any situations in which you have got your own way despite some resistance from others. Why do you think you were successful? Think about any occasions on which you have been involved in a debate, or other activity involving influencing skills such as charitable fund-raising.

Networking

This is the fancy word for nurturing useful relationships with other people. Generally it is also about building and maintaining productive working relationships. To be a good networker you need to be able to approach people you do not know, put them at their ease and develop a meaningful dialogue.

▨ Try to remember a time when you deliberately widened your circle of acquaintances, especially to include people you would not normally have contact with because of different interests or beliefs. How did you make contact? How do you maintain the relationship? What have you learnt?

Conflict resolution

This sounds a bit extreme, but the ability to deal with controversy, negativity, disputes and confrontation is an important skill. In many situations people will actively object, for example, to new ways of doing things, or disagree with the way they are being organised or what they are being asked to do.

▨ Do people approach you to mediate when they have an argument? Are you able to defuse difficult situations? Have you ever had to cope with angry customers? Consider what verbal and non-verbal skills you have that help to calm people down and move disagreements in a more positive direction.

Sensitivity

Sensitivity in this sense means showing consideration for others, having concern for their anxieties and feelings (empathy), demonstrating an interest in their opinions even if you do not agree with them, and being tolerant of the different needs that people have.

■ Think about a time when you made the effort to appreciate a different group of people, culture or lifestyle, especially if it made you confront your preconceptions or re-evaluate the way you deal with people. If you are involved in any community or social support activities, how have these changed your outlook?

Communication skills

Communication skills concern being able to write in a clear, fluent and grammatically correct way, having the ability to present information effectively, and to be able to use word processors and related technology.

Writing

It is essential that you can express yourself on paper. You must know how to structure verbal arguments and be able to tailor what you write to the needs of the recipient. While you will not necessarily be expected to know how to write something like a business plan or project proposal, you will be expected to be able to write a letter, evaluate a number of pieces of written information and produce a précis, and write a simple report.

■ Your academic career may well have involved you in writing essays, reporting on projects or producing dissertations. What have you done? How did you plan and implement any writing assignments? Have you

written stories or articles in your spare time? Have you
written for a newsletter, student newspaper, academic
journal or similar?

Presenting

This is the preparation and illustrative parts of giving a presentation. There is skill involved in making the right sort of notes
for a presentation and in organising support material. In addition, effective presentations often involve the use of audio-
visual equipment.

▓ Again, recall an occasion on which you had to give a
presentation. What did you do to give the talk greater
impact? Did you use slides, video or prepare overhead
transparencies? How did you prepare the content?
Can you use computer packages such as Microsoft
PowerPoint™? Can you set up and use audio equipment?

Computer literacy

Computer skills are highly valued in the labour market. Even
in non-graduate jobs people who have basic skills earn about
15 per cent more than those who do not use computers at all.
In the graduate context employers expect familiarity, at the
very least, with word processing packages, the Internet and
e-mail.

▓ Most degree-level courses require work to be prepared
using a word processor. Make a list of any other
computer applications and programs with which
you are familiar: for example, presentation and
graphics packages, spreadsheets, databases, statistics
packages, programming languages and Web authoring
tools.

Self-organisation skills

There is a long list here that includes being reliable and able to cope with pressure, having good planning and time management skills, plus flexibility and the desire to work hard and take responsibility (achievement 'motivation').

Reliability

The world of work requires people who are disciplined, work hard, take responsibility and meet deadlines. In fact it is all about delivering the right results at the right time; it is not about setting your own agenda and only completing jobs when you feel like it.

▓ Employers often complain that graduates do not know what it is like to do a proper day's work. If you are to counter this view you need to provide ongoing examples of reliable working practices. If you have a part-time job this will obviously help; otherwise provide evidence of academic projects completed on time, disciplined revision for examinations and so forth.

Resilience

Another feature of work is that there are inevitable set-backs, projects that go wrong and people who complain. To survive in the long term you must be able to cope with pressure, especially in jobs where there is a great deal of customer or client-facing activity.

▓ Identify a recent event that placed you under stress. What effect did it have? How did you cope? Did it affect your performance? Generally, how do you deal with stressful situations? How do you unwind/relax after a stressful day?

Planning

Planning involves the production of schedules and timetables, time management and attention to detail. The skilled planner establishes priorities and visualises what will be needed to fulfil future requirements.

▓ Think of a number of different situations where you have had to be particularly organised. How did you plan the detailed parts of the project or exercise? How did you make sure it was done on time? How did you take into account future needs and requirements?

Flexibility

In order to deal with change you need to be able to manage work tasks in a flexible way. It is also important to adopt a flexible style with others when necessary, to take their views into account and to adapt your approach when appropriate.

▓ How do you cope when you have to change your approach midway through doing something? Do you find it easy to change course or do you resist? Make a list of situations where you discovered that changing your approach was actually the answer. What did you learn?

Achievement orientation

Achievement does not sound like a skill, but a willingness to work enthusiastically towards targets, to be an initiator rather than a follower, and to be able to make decisions is a quality that employers prize.

▓ Think of occasions when you have taken the lead or assumed responsibility. What were the circumstances? How did you do it? What was the effect? Have you ever set up a club, society or group from scratch? How did you get things going? How did you enlist support? What has happened since?

Thinking skills

As a graduate it will be taken as read that you learn quickly, identify and solve problems, pull out ideas from disorganised information and draw the correct conclusions, and think of new ways of doing things.

Learning

Learning as a skill does not just mean attending courses, reading books and browsing the literature on a particular subject; rather it implies that you actively identify your learning needs and apply what you have learnt in the workplace. In this sense it is an active and skilful activity, not a passive one.

■ This sort of learning is about rapidly absorbing new information, remembering it, and applying it in new situations. When have you done this? What did you apply your learning to? How are you keeping up to date in this new area?

Problem solving

Problem solving has two parts: analysis and solution. Problem analysis involves identifying a problem, breaking it down into its constituent parts, working out how they fit together and identifying the reasons why there is a problem in the first place. Solution concerns the generation of possible answers and the use of appropriate techniques to bring about a remedy.

■ Try to think of a time when you were faced with a difficult problem, be it academic, personal or work-related. How did you find out what the problem was?

What techniques did you use to try to solve it? How successful were you?

Conceptualising

This is an intellectual skill that involves the accumulation and processing of information in order to discover new concepts or generate new ways of looking at things. It is a skill that is invaluable in all forms of research activity or situations that require a theoretical understanding.

■ If you are good at discussing hypothetical issues, and quick to identify the main themes, you have this skill. List some recent examples. Why do you think you are good at this? What is it about the way that you think that helps you to get to the crux of an argument? How do you generate new ideas?

Judgement

Judgement is an analytical ability concerned with making sensible decisions or proposals based on a consideration of all the facts and options available. One can also say that it is about coming to rational conclusions and being discriminating in what you do.

■ Look back on some decisions that you have made and subsequently had to change. Why did you have to change your mind? Now consider a situation where there were a number of options and you came to the 'right' decision. Why did you get it right?

Creativity

Creativity is notoriously difficult to define. However, it is concerned with producing imaginative or original ideas and proposals. It also encompasses the process of building and expanding on existing ideas, and a breaking away from the 'traditional' or 'tried-and-tested' way of doing things.

▓ Have you ever invented anything? What? How did you come to invent it? Does it work? Do you consider yourself to be a creative problem solver? Why? Are you able to improve on other people's ideas?

Other transferable skills

An obvious omission from the above list is leadership, but this is not a single skill, rather a combination of factors such as the ability to motivate and develop other people, give direction, empower and stimulate. Likewise there are the 'skills' of initiative, tenacity and integrity. However, the aim of this chapter is not to give an exhaustive list, as this could easily cover 50 different skills, but to direct you to the four main clusters and some of the most important. You may also have noticed that the definition of a skill appears to be quite broad. Some actually are distinct skills; others are more like values or aspects of personality.

Unfortunately there is considerable fuzziness in this area. Interest and motivation also play a big part in whether or not you apply your skills. Take numerical ability as an example. It is perfectly possible to have a great deal of numerical aptitude and be no good at mathematics. That is because in order to apply numerical ability you need to have learnt what to do. So raw numerical ability is of little use if it has not been developed, and to develop it you need to have been interested in maths in the first place. The moral is that you may have a number of latent abilities, but to develop the skills that go with them takes effort!

Action steps

▓ Make a list of your transferable skills and decide how you will describe or demonstrate them to an employer. You also need to consider what do to about any areas of potential weakness.

▓ A self-development tool (computer disk) called Skills Tracker is available from the National Centre for Work Experience, 344-54 Grays Inn Road, London WC1X 8BP. This will help you organise your skills and work out what to put on application forms and say at interviews.

▓ Working out your transferable skills will take time. Don't try to avoid this part of your career planning. Many employers leave vacancies unfilled rather than recruit graduates without the skills they need.

Personality

Personality plays an influential role in how you relate to other people and perform in a job. It is usually quite well developed by early adulthood, and while it can change over the years that follow, it rarely changes much. For example, if you are basically an outgoing sort of person you are extremely unlikely to change into a quiet introvert. However, that is not to say that you will not learn a whole series of coping mechanisms along the way: these are behaviours that allow you to act 'out of character' when required. So if you are an extrovert you will need to be quiet and thoughtful on occasions, or adopt the style of an introvert; likewise if you are an introvert you will probably have to be more assertive and direct from time to time, or take on the mantle of the extrovert. The only problem with coping mechanisms is that some people are more skilled than others, and it takes considerable energy to project a new image. In consequence it is important that you understand the ways in which you prefer to interact with other people. Your 'natural' style will be a far more comfortable one to assume in the work situation.

There are well over 20,000 words in the English language that describe aspects of personality. However, many of these describe similar characteristics, and indeed psychologists now agree that there are five main personality dimensions. These are often known as the 'big five' and concern how people behave towards others (relating), approach new situations (action), control their emotions (feelings), regulate their actions (conformity), and the way in which they reason (thinking). More specifically they can be described as:

- **Extroversion – introversion.** The classic extrovert is sociable, persuasive, energetic, demonstrative and emotional. He or she may also be opinionated, impulsive and unreliable. In contrast introverts are often quiet, thoughtful and restrained.
- **Tough-mindedness – tender-mindedness.** The truly tough-minded individual is insensitive, assertive and concentrates on the task at hand. His tender-minded cousin is warm, caring, considerate and sensitive. In a nutshell the former tells people what to do, the latter 'sells' a course of action.
- **Anxious – relaxed.** A certain amount of anxiety is perfectly normal; however, if you are a naturally anxious person you are likely to be tense, cautious and pessimistic, as opposed to the relaxed person who is characteristically calm, accepting and optimistic.
- **Independent – conforming.** The independently-minded character is often unconventional, experimental and dislikes rules and regulations. The conformist, on the other hand, is conservative, down to earth, moderate and conventional.
- **Organised – informal.** A highly organised person is generally precise, thorough, self-controlled and intolerant of people who are disorganised! Those who are disorganised are often informal, tolerant and casual in approach.

Of course personality can be described in far more precise terms, but it is useful to consider your own personality in light of the main dimensions. It is also important to recognise that there is no single 'right' personality for a job, and that employers are often looking for a range of different people. Additionally you should consider that employers associate skills, such as the transferable skills we looked at earlier, with personality characteristics. For instance:

▓ If you are a warm, tender-minded person who is good at responding to other people you will be assumed to have good spoken communication skills.

▓ A person who is thorough and organised and uses tried-and-tested ways of doing things will often be assumed to have good planning skills.

▓ The tough-minded extrovert who is determined, forceful and task-focused will be assumed to have good influencing skills.

So an important step in understanding yourself and the jobs to which you will be suited is to define your own personality.

Action steps

▓ Complete a personality questionnaire. There are many well-designed questionnaires that you can use to get an accurate picture of your own personality. Ask your university or college careers service for help.

▓ If you have difficulty getting hold of a questionnaire there are a number of books you can purchase. Look out for *How to Master Personality Questionnaires* (Mark Parkinson, published by *The Times*/Kogan Page, London, 2000). You will also find interactive questionnaires on the Internet: type the words 'personality' or 'psychometrics' into a search engine.

▓ Assess your own personality against the five dimensions described. For example, are you essentially an extrovert, an introvert or a bit of both? When you have considered all the dimensions ask a friend, or a number of friends, to assess you in the same way. Do you agree? Who do you think is the more accurate?

Work experience

If you are a mature student you may already have appropriate work experience. If you are not, you need to think about how to present any jobs you have had, 'year-out' experience or placement activities in the most effective manner. For example, if you have worked in a student bar you will have learnt how to cooperate with other people (teamwork), take and act on customer orders (customer service), calculate the price of a round of drinks (numeracy), deal with people who have drunk too much (communication), handle complaints (sensitivity) and so on. In a similar way if you have been on any form of placement you should be able to describe what you did, the skills you learnt and how you contributed to your employer's organisation. The trick is to think beyond the repetitive, mundane (and possibly boring) jobs you have done and recognise what you have learnt. Remember that employers are interested in recruiting people who have made an effort to find work and develop their skills, especially if these demonstrate customer orientation and business awareness.

Recruiters also favour candidates who have taken time out before going to college or university. Those who have been out in the world are considered to have a better idea about what work involves and to have more common sense. However, this does not mean that lying on a beach for a year, before or after university, is a good move. Your time must be seen to have been spent constructively. So things like a TEFL (Teaching English as a Foreign Language) course, an expedition or volunteering on a Third World project are what is required. They suggest that you have initiative, have probably had to raise money, are flexible, practical, and are able to communicate and build relationships.

Action steps

■ Make a list of all the different sorts of work you have done over the last few years. Full-time or part-time? Voluntary? Working on a kibbutz? Sports or tourism related? Summer camps? Au pairing? What did you achieve? What skills did you develop?

■ Have you taken a specialist course, while studying, that will help you to get work? TEFL? Computing? Statistics? Be prepared to talk about what you have learnt to an employer.

■ If you have no work experience, is there time to get some? Remember, if you have work experience it puts you at an advantage compared to those who don't.

Putting it all together

If you have worked through this chapter systematically you should have information on your interests, values and motivations. This will help you to identify the sort of jobs that you would like to explore. On the other side of the equation you should have generated lists of abilities, transferable skills, personality characteristics and work experience. This is what you have to sell an employer. However, all this information can be somewhat overwhelming, and at times difficult to prioritise.

One way of making sense of job options versus skills, abilities and so forth is to produce a job match grid. This is an at-a-glance technique that provides a way of evaluating your options from where they lie on a grid.

How to do it

▓ Pick the five jobs that you think best fit your interests.

▓ Allocate a mark to each job based on your interests, values and motivations:

> **Interests:** 1 = I would do it if I had to.
>
> 2 = I am quite interested.
>
> 3 = I don't mind one way or the other.
>
> 4 = I am definitely interested.
>
> 5 = I want to do this job.

Values and motivations: Use the five values and motivations that you identified earlier to 'test' the job. For example, if you think it would meet all five of your main sources of motivation, give it a '5'; only four, give it a '4', and so on. Do the same thing for values.

▓ Now allocate one more mark to each job based on your willingness to undertake further study or complete professional training. Such training usually takes a number of years.

> **Training:** 1 = I do not wish to undertake any further studying/training.
>
> 2 = I would rather not do any more studying/training.
>
> 3 = I don't mind one way or the other.
>
> 4 = I would quite like to do further studying/training.
>
> 5 = I would definitely like to study/train further.

▓ Add the four numbers together for each job. This is the job score. (The maximum possible is 20.)

▓ Now look at your **current abilities, transferable skills, personality** and **work experience** (capabilities). As before, you have five marks to allocate to each depending on how closely you think you would fit the job requirements.

▓ Allocate marks for each area in the following way:

    1 = No match with my capabilities.

    2 = A small degree of overlap with my capabilities.

    3 = My capabilities mean I could probably do this job.

    4 = I could almost definitely do this job.

    5 = My capabilities ideally suit me to this job.

■ Add the four numbers together for each job. This is the match score. (The maximum possible is 20.)

■ If you have not already done so, give each job a label. You can do this by allocating a letter. For example 'A' is personnel manager, 'B' is psychologist, 'C' is careers adviser, and so on.

■ Get some graph paper and draw a box 20 units wide by 20 units deep.

■ Across the top of the grid write 'Jobs' and down the side write 'Match'.

■ Add a 20 point scale: see the example that follows.

Example

Helen has completed the exercise and obtained the following scores:

Table 2.1

	Job	*Match*	
A)	personnel manager	17	10
B)	occupational psychologist	18	20
C)	careers adviser	14	16
D)	market researcher	6	13
E)	teacher	10	8

Just looking at the figures we can see that Helen likes the idea of the job of personnel manager but is a moderate match; she also likes occupational psychology and is an excellent match;

dislikes market research, but this is a better match than personnel manager, and so on.

The results can also be presented graphically by using them as coordinates on the grid. Using this system, the closer a job is to the top right-hand corner the better it fits your interests and current capabilities.

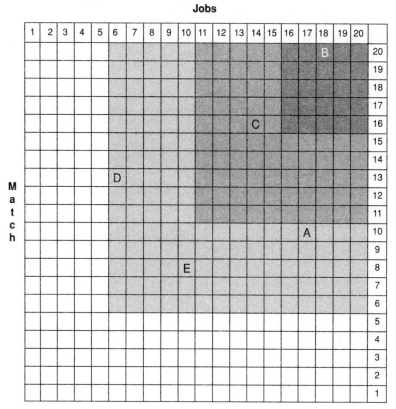

Figure 2.1 *Job match grid*

Other resources

Your university or college careers service can always help you to produce a career plan. Even if you have graduated, many will still be able to offer you career planning workshops and access to computer-based guidance systems. One of the best graduate systems is called *Prospects Planner*. It will help you to find out what you are good at, what will interest you, which careers suit you (it includes a database of information on over 400 graduate jobs), your chances of getting into these careers, and how to make effective applications. The computer program can be used without supervision but you will need to make a significant time commitment to get the most out of it.

For those of you who prefer to read books, the following offer valuable advice:

Barrie Hopson and Mike Scally, *Build your own Rainbow* (Management Books, Chalford, Glos., 1999).
Richard Bolles, *What Color is Your Parachute?* (10 Speed Press, Berkeley, California, published annually).

Personal summary

When you need to compile a CV, complete an application form or prepare for an interview, you will find it useful to have a personal summary at hand. Draw up a table on a piece of paper, and create and complete the following sections:

Job ideas

- ▓ Job titles (jobs that attract me):

- ▓ Interests (my people/information/things interests):

- ▓ Values (my five key values):

■ Motivation (my five motivational factors):

■ Other important characteristics (location, environment etc):

■ Achievements (things I would like to achieve):

Personal strengths

■ Abilities (abstract, verbal, numerical, other):

■ Transferable skills (main areas of expertise):

■ Personality ('big five' analysis):

■ Work experience (details and skills acquired):

■ Knowledge (special work-related knowledge):*

■ Development potential (things I would like to learn):

*Note: You may have gained this through working, or it may be the product of studying a vocational course.

3

Finding the right job

The key to finding a good graduate job is to understand how the job market works. In particular, you need to appreciate that there are a number of ways in which you can find a job. These include traditional sources such as newspapers and magazines, special recruitment events laid on for students, and increasingly these days, job opportunities posted on the Internet. Indeed it is now estimated that 88 per cent of final year students actively look for jobs on the net. This chapter will help you to understand how to use these different opportunities.

The jobs market

If you slice up the jobs market you find that there are direct and indirect ways of getting at jobs. The direct route usually involves responding to an advertisement placed by an employer, whereas the indirect route generally concerns job-hunting through an employment agency. In addition, jobs can be tracked down through personal contacts or job fairs (the 'milk round'), or through cold canvassing.

Most people try to get jobs through advertisements or by using agencies. However, developing your own contacts through networking, or approaching employers direct, can also be effective job-hunting strategies. That is because there are many jobs that are never advertised.

Employer tactics

From the statistics available, about two-thirds of the larger graduate employers target particular universities, with an additional 40 per cent concentrating on specific departments or courses. However, these figures are unlikely to rise significantly as employers switch their attention to Internet-based recruitment techniques. Already over 40 per cent use the Internet to advertise vacancies, with a further 20 per cent intending to do so in the near future. In addition 25 per cent already have online application forms.

It is important to realise that while employers are sensitive to the latest developments in recruitment technology, they are still likely to use what they consider to be tried and tested methods. The annual visit to a handful of universities is a good example. However, as you will see, even this is changing, not least because employers are having to respond to graduate shortages. An example is the construction industry, which is finding it difficult to recruit sufficient graduates from numerate disciplines. In consequence what is essentially a very conservative industry is having to cast its net much wider, and to seriously consider the value that any well-educated graduate can bring.

To maximise your chances of landing a good job you need to be aware of the latest recruitment trends and to respond to them.

Advertised jobs

Jobs are advertised in newspapers and journals, employer

directories and on the Internet. Your university or college careers service will also have access to lists of vacancies.

Newspapers can be good sources of vacancies, but you must realise that if you are dealing with a national daily the competition for any advertised jobs is likely to be intense. In consequence it might be better to look in more specialised publications. For example, if you are interested in a career in science, you could try the appointments section of the *New Scientist*. You should also pay attention to trade or professional journals, especially those that are only available to members of particular societies or associations. For example, if you want to become a psychologist you can look in the Appointments Memorandum that accompanies the journal, *The Psychologist*. If you want to enter the retail sector, then *The Grocer* is a good place to look, and so on.

Returning to newspapers for a moment, do not forget to look in local papers. In many areas these carry graduate jobs, as employers with regional offices often recruit locally. As a point of strategy you also need to check the papers on the right day. National newspapers carry different sorts of vacancy on different days of the week, and often have special graduate sections. For instance, it is well worth looking at *The Times Appointments*, and also *The Guardian*, which carries jobs throughout the week, and has a graduate section on each Thursday, plus a useful section called 'Rise' on Saturday. The lesson to learn is that you must check the right sections, and not expect to find your ideal job (at least at the start of your career) amongst the top management positions advertised in *The Sunday Times*!

Action steps

▨ Make a habit of reading the national newspapers, including the business sections. This will help you to spot adverts and may also provide useful background information for interviews.

- Produce a list of which papers advertise the jobs that interest you, and on which days. In most cases you will find that the paper produces a key to its job adverts for the week in each edition.
- If you are studying a vocational or professional course find out if your professional body publishes a magazine containing job opportunities. Look in the library and ask the careers staff.

Employer directories such as *GET* are published each year and contain details on thousands of different employers. They tell you about the sorts of job on offer and details of training, salary, what the employer is looking for, and how to apply. Hobsons Publishing plc, who produce *GET*, also issue a series of *Casebooks* that gives employment details for particular employment sectors.

Example: Renault UK

The Year 2000 edition of the *Marketing, Retailing and Sales Casebook* has two pages dedicated to Renault UK. The introduction says that Renault are looking for high calibre graduates and that:

> Your qualifications are important, but we are also interested in your personality, drive and commitment. We require individuals who know a bit about the world and what makes it work. Your ability to demonstrate strategic thinking will go a long way in shaping your career.

It goes on to say that they are recruiting in marketing, sales, finance and retail, and that they have offices in Harefield, Middlesex and Swindon. They are interested in graduates with degrees in business studies, economics, management science and marketing, who have obtained at least six months' commercial experience. A good command of oral and written French is required. There are 4–5 vacancies and the starting salary is £18,000 plus a company car. After 12 months' training, graduates will be expected to take up a junior management position. The section concludes with details on how to make an application, by initially talking to a named person in the Professional Pre-Selection Services department. Information is also provided on the deadline for applications, and that interviews usually take place in March and are followed by an invitation to a graduate assessment centre. Successful candidates join the company in September.

Obviously the requirements and number of vacancies vary between employers. In the same edition Abbey National plc were looking for 100 graduates. Directories and Casebooks are issued free and can be obtained from your university or college careers service. There are special *Casebooks* for 'Career Women', and publications for ethnic minority graduates such as *Kaleidoscope* produced by Arberry Pink Ltd. You can obtain further information from the Hobsons Web site at: www.get.hobsons.com.

Action steps

- ▓ Visit your careers service and collect all the relevant free directories. You should be able to find *GET* (as mentioned) and the *Prospects Directory*, published by CSU.
- ▓ Collect any other publications that cover your particular areas of interest. Again you will find *Casebooks* covering things like *Marketing*, *Retailing and Sales* (Hobsons), the *Focus On* series from CSU, as well as those covering jobs in Europe such as *Target Europe* from GTI.
- ▓ Gather and download additional information from employer Web sites (the addresses will be in your directories), and visit other useful sites such as the Hobsons site and Prospects Web: www.prospects. csu.ac.uk.

Internet Web sites carry large numbers of vacancies and other useful job-hunting information. Many newspapers maintain Web sites which publish the same job vacancies as are contained in the paper. They have the advantage that it is easier to look for jobs because you can automatically search by job type, location and salary. The best Web sites are operated by *The Times*, www.the-times.co.uk/appointments, *The Guardian*, www.jobsunlimited.co.uk, and *The Independent*, www.independent.co.uk.

Employers also have their own Web sites, and some even have special graduate Web sites. For example Lloyds TSB have developed a dedicated graduate site (www.lloydstsbgraduate. co.uk) that contains information about the company, the graduates who already work there, and training programmes. There is also a downloadable version of their application form and details on their selection procedures.

In addition there are a host of general recruitment Web sites that cater for graduates. These include sections of the big Web sites such as the Campus Zone at www.monster.com, or Topgrads at www.topjobs.co.uk, as well as those solely targeted at graduates. Web sites such as these, for example www.milkround.co.uk, provide a range of job-hunting and information services. Typically these include:

▓ **Employer profiles.** These are detailed portraits of employers and the careers they have on offer.
▓ **Sector profiles.** In-depth careers information on key industrial sectors, such as retailing, engineering and IT.
▓ **Immediate vacancies.** A listing of the jobs that are currently available through the site.
▓ **Careers advice.** How to make successful job applications, deal with interviews, cope with psychometric tests and so on.
▓ **CV database.** A system for creating and storing a CV in the site database. (Your CV is then made available to potential employers.)

■ **E-mail notification.** An automatic e-mail system that advises you of any vacancies that meet your requirements.

The top ten graduate job Web sites

There are at least 250 major recruitment Web sites dealing with vacancies in the UK. The list grows longer by the day. However, the Web sites that are most frequently rated as offering a high quality service to graduates are:

■ Activate: www.activatecareers.co.uk (available on CD ROM)
■ Doctor Job: www.doctorjob.co.uk
■ Gradrecruit: www.gradrecruit.co.uk
■ Graduate Base: www.graduatebase.com
■ Graduate Recruitment: www.graduate-recruitment. co.uk
■ Gradnet: www.gradunet.co.uk
■ Jobsearch online: www.jobsearch-online.co.uk
■ Just People: www.justpeople.com
■ Milk Round: www.milkround.co.uk
■ Prospects: www.prospects.csu.ac.uk

Other specialist Web sites are worth a visit as well. For example www.careerfever.co.uk is a 'virtual reality' system which allows students to 'visit' employers and take virtual interviews. As the graphics are of such high quality a CD ROM supports the system, and this is distributed free of charge to all final-year students. Another interesting site is www.hotrecruit.co.uk. This is a temporary work recruitment site which offers thousands of national and international jobs. One of the unusual aspects of the site is a 'crazy jobs' section, for those who want to avoid the more tedious forms of temporary work! This includes 'jobs' such as sperm donor, Father Christmas and tequila girl. For the more scientific and technically minded there is www. insidecareers.co.uk which focuses on actuarial, accountancy, engineering, IT, logistics, management consultancy and tax adviser jobs.

If you intend to surf the Internet for a job you need to make sure that you are dealing with reputable organisations. Make sure that the site includes the operators' telephone number and address. Check the vacancies to see how many they offer and how recent they are. Are there any reassurances given about what they will do with your personal details? Who will be able to view your CV (if you submit one)? Are you asked to pay? If in doubt you can check with the Recruitment and Employment Confederation. You will find their Web site at www.rec.uk.com. The most important thing to remember is that employers pay for recruitment services, you don't. If you are asked to pay for a service, treat the Web site with caution.

Action steps

■ Get to know the Web sites that deal with graduate jobs. Start with the list provided, but also use your search engine to find any new sites.

■ If you don't have your own computer, visit a cyber café or other access point and explore the possibilities. Remember that most students now look for jobs on the net.

■ Try submitting your details to a few sites and see what you get back. You can do this even if you have not yet graduated, just put in your degree subject and likely grade.

Careers services offer graduates a great deal of useful support and information. You can access employer vacancy lists and collect the latest job magazines such as *Prospects Today* (published by CSU Ltd). They can also put you in contact with employer organisations, and most stock up-to-date brochures and application forms. In addition many careers services organise careers fairs. These are held each year for finalists and provide an ideal opportunity to meet employers and find out what they have on offer – see 'Job fairs and networking'.

Additional information on university and college careers services can be obtained from the Association of Graduate Careers Advisory Services at www.agcas.csu.ac.uk.

Making sense of adverts

You have found an advert that you think describes your ideal job. But what does it all mean? If you look at enough graduate adverts you will see that they usually beak down into five main segments:

Job title, salary and location

Obviously the job title will depend on the job but it will often be something like 'graduate trainee', 'graduate manager', 'marketing graduate' or 'graduate sales trainee'. Of course it might also just say 'graduate opportunities' or be replaced by an eye-catching headline. For example the leading graduate recruitment agency, Pareto Law, recently ran an advert featuring a glass full of frothy lager with the headline, 'Nobody likes big heads... but we're looking for the cream.'

In many cases directly under the title will be an indication of salary. This will say something like '£17,500 + benefits package' or 'c. £18,000 + car + bonus'. In the first case the starting salary is £17,500 and the benefits will usually include things like a pension, medical insurance, staff concessions on goods and services (if appropriate), subsidised canteen, sports facilities and so forth. In the second example a company car is included and a monetary bonus is payable to good performers. However, the vital part to spot is the small 'c' before the salary figure. This means that the salary is 'circa', or in the region of

£18,000. In reality the employer is telling you that you will start on £18,000 plus or minus 5 to 10 per cent, depending on how keen they are to employ you. Another prefix to look out for is OTE, as in 'OTE £30K'. This stands for 'on target earnings' or 'opportunity to earn' and is often found in adverts for sales jobs. As the definitions imply, it means that if you meet all your targets you will earn £30,000; if you don't, you won't!

There is nothing mysterious about the location part of the opening text, although it may be rather vague and say something like 'Opportunities nationwide'. But in most cases it will just say 'London' or 'Southeast' (London plus the Home Counties), 'West Midlands', or whatever.

The company
This is the marketing pitch, and virtually all adverts will try to convince you that Company X or Organisation Y is the best in the land. However, bear in mind that they will all claim to be market-leading award winners with impeccable ethical standards and overjoyed customers. A real example:

> Company X is one of the world's leading engineering companies with a truly global presence and an international reputation. We have a £10 billion turnover and employ 60,000 personnel worldwide. Our reputation as an employer and commitment to our customers is second to none. Now there is a chance for you to start your career with us and share in the future success of our company.

At this stage you need to ask yourself if you have ever heard of them. If the above was an advert placed by British Aerospace, then the answer is probably 'yes'; but if it describes Sealand Engineering, the answer is undoubtedly 'no'. So are you really dealing with a large and successful company? What do you know about its reputation? Have you read anything in the press about them? Are they considered to be a good employer? (See 'Cold canvassing' for details on how to research employers.)

The position

The next part of the advert describes the job. It will usually
contain details on your role and responsibilities, and opportunities for training and development. Depending on the position
some descriptions will be very technical, and some quite vague:

> You will be responsible for the design, installation and support of appli-
> cations that are essential for the functionality of the customer's business
> processes. The systems that you will produce will be developed in a C++
> environment. As a key member of the project team, you will be expected
> to produce detailed specifications based upon customer requirements,
> develop and test software and install and commission on site.
>
> (Witron (software engineer))

> Join the Security Service and you'll play a key part in protecting society
> from terrorism, espionage, the proliferation of weapons of mass destruc-
> tion and other threats to national security.
>
> (HM Security Service (MI5 officer))

Whatever you think of the job description, you must make sure
that the employer is offering an attractive training scheme (see
below). This is an important part of the employment package
and will make a big difference when you come to change jobs
in the future. If there is no hint of training it may be wise to
think again about applying for the job.

> We're a business where training, opportunity and reward put real
> achievement within reach... We currently have places on our Supply
> Chain Management Training Scheme... the scheme is designed to
> provide the opportunity to acquire strong technical, operational and
> management skills through practical hands-on work, projects and
> specialist training.
>
> (Sainsbury's)

> National Grid's Graduate Development Programme boasts outstanding
> opportunities reflecting our dynamic status. During our 18-month
> programme you will gain first-hand experience in your chosen field,
> working on valuable and exciting projects... we provide sponsorship
> towards a professional qualification.
>
> (National Grid)

Note: In case you are wondering, the Security Services do provide training, described as 'a blend of formal courses and on-the-job training'.

About you

A particular degree is required for some jobs, and if this is the case it will be specified here. If the position is open to all graduates, it will say that there is no preferred degree discipline. The rest of the copy will describe the ideal candidate:

> You'll have the intellectual stamina and interpersonal skills to thrive in an unpredictable, exciting environment. Above all else, you'll be eager for direct involvement in international issues.
>
> (HM Diplomatic Service (Diplomat))

> We are look for people who are self-motivated and enthusiastic. Graduates who can innovate and challenge, learn fast and deliver.
>
> (Marconi (all graduate positions))

> You'll need some tangible assets; an agile and analytical mind, a good head for figures, an appetite for tax and legal matters, sound business awareness and well developed interpersonal skills.
>
> (Arthur Anderson ('human capital' specialist))

> You'll need a flair for fashion and an understanding of how catwalk styles and colour translate into our customers' expectations... you'll need the commercial awareness to make objective decisions. It is vitally important that you're a well organised team player who can build positive and productive working relationships.
>
> (British Home Stores (fashion buyer))

> You'll be a dynamic self-starter with bags of energy; innovative and lively, you will have demonstrable flair for identifying sales opportunities and bringing these to fruition. The ability to work without supervision and the desire to influence future developments is crucial.
>
> (Pearson Education (sales position))

In addition you will find that employers often ask for language skills, a willingness to relocate to a different part of the country, or even internationally, and for relevant work experience. The good news is that there are probably very few people who could live up to the expectations generated by most adverts. However, you must fulfil the general requirements, and it is at this stage that a thorough knowledge of your abilities, transferable skills, values, career drivers (motivation) and personality will pay dividends.

How to apply

This is the bit that describes the mechanics of how to apply for the job. It will advise you to send your CV to a particular address, to send for an application form (submit a standard application form – see Chapter 4), or apply through a named Web site. Many of the larger organisations encourage applications via the Internet, and for some it is the only method of application.

The advert will often be supported by graphics that have been designed to catch your attention. Those that you see on Web sites may even incorporate moving images and sound. In fact some adverts are really quite beautiful. But you should realise that adverts are mostly prepared for employers by specialist agencies. The fact that the advert looks great does not necessarily mean that the job opportunity is equally good. Tread carefully and read all the adverts that appear to fit your requirements, not just the flashy ones.

Agencies and executive search

For many the main 'indirect' route to a job is to sign up with an employment agency. You will find plenty in your local high street, and many more tucked away in offices behind the scenes. Look in the Yellow Pages or the local newspaper for details. The larger agencies also have their own Web sites, for example the Reed site is at www.reed.co.uk/graduate.

If you are dealing with a professional agency you should expect to have a personal interview with an employment consultant who will make a note of your interests. You will also need to complete a number of forms and questionnaires, and you may be asked to take some psychometric tests (see Chapter 5). Once the consultant has gathered sufficient information you will be given an overview of the sort of employers they deal with, and the vacancies they currently have on their books. If you are attracted to any of the jobs, the consultant will forward your details to the employer and arrange interviews on your behalf.

Which agency, or agencies, you select to act on your behalf is purely a matter of personal preference. That being said, ensure that you feel comfortable with the consultant(s) and the service offered. If you don't feel like a valued customer, walk away and find another agency. Likewise if the agency asks for money, find a new one. The reason you should avoid paying for the services of an employment agency is that they make their money from the employer. The rates can vary, but they will probably receive a fee based on somewhere between 15 and 25 per cent of your annual salary if they successfully place you in a job.

Head-hunters

When companies are looking for 'hard to find' employees or senior managers they often employ the services of an executive search agency. Colloquially these are known as 'head-hunters'. They operate in a slightly different way from traditional employment agencies, in that they deal with fewer (higher-value) positions and offer a far more personal service. In addition you don't walk into a headhunters' office, they come and find you!

The idea of head-hunting graduates is very new and is a response to the massive expansion in higher education, and consequently the number of graduates. It is now impossible for employers to send recruiters to every campus, and so they have to be far more precise in their approach.

In order to get spotted you will need to have a high profile and be an exceptional student or graduate. Even then an approach is not guaranteed, as it depends on whether a head-hunting company visits the university or college. If it does, course or personal tutors usually identify high-flyers. The next step is a screening interview, followed by a more in-depth interview, before being introduced to the head-hunter's client. The entire process can take some time, but it is a way of being placed with a firm you would probably never have considered joining.

Action steps

- ▓ Research the agencies in your local area and find out which specialise in the jobs that interest you.
- ▓ Visit plenty of different agencies and compare their services. Deal with as many as you feel comfortable; there is no limit to how many you can use.
- ▓ Ask your university or college careers service if they ever have dealings with executive search agencies. It is always worth enquiring!

Job fairs and networking

Historically employers used to visit universities and take part in an annual recruitment event called the 'milk round'. For many final-year students this was the main source of contact with employers, and vice versa. However, over the years the milk round has been in decline, not least because many employers are now recruiting throughout the year and only concentrating on a small number of institutions: a policy designed to cream off the best candidates before their competitors secure their services. The facts that students have more to do in terms of course work, and even part-time jobs, have also made it difficult to concentrate recruitment into one single event.

The response to the decline of the milk round has been the rise of the recruitment fair. These are events sponsored by newspapers and large recruiters which are designed to attract graduates from all over the country. For example, the *Guardian*-sponsored Autumn Graduate Recruitment Fair, held in Olympia, features some 40 blue-chip employers covering all the main employment sectors, and attracts some 7,000 final-year students and graduates. Admission is free, and those who visit can also attend presentations and CV workshops. Similar events are held throughout the country and the number of fairs is increasing each year.

Fairs attract many thousands of visitors and can be quite bewildering if you don't prepare yourself.

Action steps

- ■ Check the press for details of forthcoming fairs, especially location and admission times.
- ■ Make sure that you know what careers interest you before attending. If you don't, you will waste a great deal of time.
- ■ Identify in advance those companies/organisations you want to impress. You may have to book a slot for an exploratory interview.

Weaving a net

Job fairs represent an active way of looking for jobs, but are really just a version of old-fashioned networking. That is introducing yourself to people who may be able to give you a job or suggest somebody else who will be able to help you in your career quest. Whether you are successful at using networking depends entirely on how much effort you put in. To be effective you need to identify at least six influential people who are known to you or your family. They might be employers themselves, or professionals such as accountants or solicitors, or just friends. The next step is to contact them and to ask each one to introduce you to somebody else who may be able to help. For example, an employer contact may not have a vacancy but probably knows of a customer or supplier that does, and so on. This might sound like a lot of effort, and it is often difficult to know where to start, but it is a way into the 'unadvertised' jobs market. This is reckoned to account for up to 30 per cent of jobs.

Another variation on the theme is the development of student conference call organisations. These are Web site and telephone-based networks designed to attract those who would not normally attend the usual recruitment events. One such organisation, DiversityNow, operates across 55 British universities, and is designed to appeal to ethnic and minority groups. Many of the big employers such as Arthur Anderson, Unilever and Vodafone are enthusiastic supporters.

To use the service it is necessary to register your details on the Web site (www.diversitynow.net), visit the conference call page and e-mail employers you would like to hear from. You are given a PIN number and a time to dial. When you dial in you join a conference call system and listen to a live presentation. You can then either just listen or ask questions using your telephone.

Action steps

- Start creating your own network of influential people. The sooner you start, the more opportunities will come your way.
- Keep a careful note of your contacts and where they come from, keep in touch, and always thank people for their help.
- If you are turned off by the idea of career fairs, and for whatever reason feel that you are going to have problems getting a job, try the conference call system.

Cold canvassing

Approaching a company 'cold' can be one of the most effective ways of getting a job, but it is also the hardest. For cold canvassing to work you must understand the jobs market and know which organisations to approach. This requires a great deal of detailed work and relies on you gathering intelligence from the business and financial press, trade and professional journals. In particular you need to make a note of any organisations for which you would like to work that are recruiting, spending large amounts of money on advertising campaigns, launching new products or services, acquiring other businesses, modernising, or in fact undergoing any sort of positive change.

When you have isolated a number of target organisations you need to gather information on their structure, culture, policy towards graduates, and most importantly of all, who makes the hiring decisions. Telephone and ask if they have corporate brochures or a company report that they can send you. Visit a reference library and look in the standard business directories such as *Kelly's* (Reed Information Services) or *Kompass*. Personnel publications such as *The Personnel Manager's Yearbook* (AP Information Services) also carry information on the top UK companies and the names and contact details for the senior managers.

The Internet is also a rich source of information. The following sites, despite some of the strange names, are worth visiting:

- Business net: www.ukbusinessnet.com
- Carols world: www.carol.co.uk
- Companies House: www.companies-house.gov.uk
- Company news: www.companynews.co.uk
- Corporate information: www.corporateinformation.com
- Corporate reports: www.corpreports.co.uk

- Financial Times: www.ft.com
- Hemmington Scott: www.hemscott.co.uk
- Kelly's Directory: www.kellys.reedinfo.co.uk

If you are interested in learning about companies with ethical policies you can find out more at www.ethical-junction.org. Additional paper-based resources include:

- *100 Best Companies to Work for in the UK* (Nightingale Media, London, 1998).
- *Britain's Best Employers* (McGraw-Hill, Maidenhead, 1999).

You can also find out about the requirements for jobs in terms of professional qualifications and training if you contact the appropriate professional body. This sort of detail is important, as you need to know what sort of training is required for particular careers and who organises it. A list of professional organisations, in CLCI (Career Library Classification Index) order, can be found on the Morrisby Web site at www.morrisby.co.uk.

When you have a clear picture of what a business does, how it is organised, who the key players are, what sort of people it recruits, what its current requirements are, who is in charge of the section that interests you and where that person is located, you are ready to apply! The application process requires a CV tailored to the organisation in question, addressed by name to the head of the department you would like to join. How to construct a suitable CV is covered in the next chapter.

Action steps

- Draw up a hit list of suitable organisations and start an 'intelligence file' on each. Use all the resources mentioned in this section.

- Fill in the background detail regarding the training and other development activities you will need to do in order to do the job well.
- Produce an individual CV for each organisation you contact. This method does not work with photocopied 'shot-gun' applications, that is, the same old CV sent to hundreds of potential employers.

Final words

Throughout this chapter the emphasis has been on finding jobs in substantial companies or large organisations. Don't forget that many graduates work in small or medium-sized enterprises and it is worth applying to these as well. The DfEE estimates that 900,000 degree holders work in enterprises employing fewer than 250 people. The other part of the employment market to consider is the voluntary sector. Remarkably, 400 or so new charities are started each year, and many of the more established employ graduates. Interestingly more men are now being attracted to the sector, which has been dominated by women for many years. The increase is probably due to the convergence of starting salaries with more commercial activities. Indeed the difference between the salary in, say, a marketing job in a large organisation and for a charity, can now be as small as 3 per cent. However, according to recruitment agencies such as Charity People (www.charitypeople.co.uk), who specialise in this area of recruitment, some prior knowledge of the voluntary sector or voluntary work is a distinct advantage.

The other option that has not been covered is postgraduate training. This is not strictly speaking 'work' in the employment sense, but students are sometimes paid for periods of work experience or for placements. In addition, some professions attract 'signing-on' payments. An example is teaching which often attracts premiums, especially in areas in which it is hard to recruit such as mathematics and physics. If you are interested in the postgraduate option there are special directories listing postgraduate courses. Much information is also available on the Internet.

4

Applying for jobs

At present there are over 70 applicants for each graduate position. This means that volume recruiters are often deluged with applications. For example, Bass plc recently received 8,500 inquiries, and processed 3,500 applications for the 30 places on its graduate recruitment programme. Bass, like other organisations, rejects most of the applications it receives. The sobering truth is that at least two-thirds are rejected at the start of the process because they do not meet the employer's requirements. This chapter is about helping to get you through the application stage to the interview.

Application forms

If you read graduate job adverts you will find a section at the end that tells you how to apply for the job. In many cases this will tell you to complete the employer's application form or a standard application form. The former may sometimes be referred to as an EAF, and the latter as a SAF. The SAF, as the name implies, is a standard format that has been agreed between all the university and college careers services and many of the largest graduate recruiters. Blank forms are available in all careers offices and can also be downloaded from the Web by visiting www.prospects.csu.ac.uk/student.

The application forms produced by employers can vary greatly in design: some are quite short, and others run to many pages. In addition, a number contain questionnaires or biodata forms (see Biodata section). However, the golden rule is to use the right sort of form for the application. Never send a SAF if an employer specifically asks you to complete their form. If the advert leaves the question open, contact the employer and ask.

Understanding forms

Whatever the design, application forms usually contain the following parts:

Contact details

This is the most straightforward part of the form as it asks for your title (Mr, Ms etc), surname and first names. Most will also allow you to show which name you prefer to be known by. Your home and term-time addresses will then be requested, with the dates you will be resident at each, plus telephone numbers and e-mail addresses.

You will be asked for your nationality and date of birth, and often whether you need a work permit for employment in the UK (and if you have one). Additional questions will include whether or not you have a full UK driving licence.

The SAF will also ask you to indicate which employer you are applying to, and your preferred 'executive' function, for example marketing or personnel.

Action steps

▦ Make sure you know where you will be living at the time your application is processed. If an employer cannot contact you, you will not get past the application stage!

■ If you have an e-mail address, use it. It is much cheaper for an employer to contact you by e-mail than send a letter.

■ For those who are not British citizens, a permit is required to work in the UK. If you apply for a permanent job you *must* have one.

Educational and work history

You will be expected to provide details of higher education, secondary education and work experience. Under 'higher education', supply accurate information on all degrees, diplomas and professional qualifications that you either already hold or expect to gain. The period of study, name of institution, title of the award with main subject areas, and result (expected or actual degree grade) will be requested. In a similar way you will need to supply details of qualifications achieved during secondary education.

For work experience you need to describe any work, whether paid or unpaid, full- or part-time, that you have done. You should supply dates, the name of the employer, your job title and responsibilities, and your main achievements.

Action steps

■ If you have qualifications other than GCSEs, A/AS-levels or their Scottish equivalents, or an international qualification like the International Baccalaureate (IB), select those that are most appropriate for the job.

■ When you give dates you only need to supply the month and year. Don't agonise over the exact day that you started or stopped doing something.

■ If you have had a job you should know what your job title and responsibilities were. List responsibilities briefly and concentrate on your achievements. An achievement is something that you learnt that helped you to be a better employee, anything else you did that increased the efficiency with which you could do your work, customers or clients you brought to the firm, or generally those things that made your employer money or improved a product or service. If there is a figure or a percentage you can quote, quote it!

Location preferences

Large employers will ask you if you have a preference for working in a particular part of the country. If you do, you can obviously provide details; however, remember that this may restrict your choice of jobs.

Interests and achievements

Typically you will be asked to describe any spare-time activities. This means activities other than things like watching television, going to the cinema or socialising. The SAF asks you to 'Include organising, leading or group activities. Those requiring initiative, creativity or giving intellectual development are also of interest.'

Other forms will often directly ask you to mention any posts of responsibility or awards that you have received. For example:

> Please list the activities, hobbies and interests that you have been involved in. Think about your role, responsibilities and achievements including scholarships, prizes and positions held.
>
> (Lloyds TSB)

The current Lloyds TSB form provides one side of A4 for you to write about your interests. This is a lot of space, and the reason that so much is provided is that employers consider non-academic interests to be a good indicator of motivation. If you think about it, extracurricular activities also provide opportunities to develop essential skills. The key to this section is to pick, say, three or four activities that span individual and team activities, as well as those that relate to work. If you have won an award so much the better, but in any case say what you have learnt and how you have developed.

Action steps

- If any of your interests are work-like, include them in this section. Employers favour those who have done more than just study.
- Most jobs involve working in teams or groups. Make sure that you describe a team activity, and if you were the leader, how you managed the role.
- Tell the truth. When you get to the interview stage you will be asked for further details.

Career choice
Inevitably you're going to have to say why you want the job. This may be probed in some detail, and as the SAF puts it, 'Offer evidence of your suitability (eg courses undertaken, work shadowing, skills, strengths and experiences). Emphasise why you consider yourself to be a strong candidate.' To answer this sort of question you must know what the job requires. You must also be able to assemble supporting evidence from your academic studies, work experience and extracurricular activities. This will take time, but you must provide a strong and positive answer.

Action steps

- Research the job. What qualities are asked for in the advert? How do these translate into everyday life? How can you show that you have them?
- Look at the employer's promotional literature. What sort of an image are they trying to promote? What sort of a culture or ethos does the organisation have? What sort of people are likely to fit in?

▓ Employers like to employ people with commitment. It is legitimate to say that you are attracted to the job because it provides security, the chance for early responsibility, opportunities for personal development and so forth. Just say why these are important to you.

Work-related abilities

This is often the hardest, and sometimes the lengthiest, part of the form. On the SAF the section is entitled 'Specific evidence' and has three parts:

▓ *Planning, implementation and achieving results.* This requires you to describe a challenging project, what you did, and how you measured your success.
▓ *Influencing, communication and teamwork.* This asks for an example of a situation where you achieved your goal by influencing the actions or opinions of others, possibly in a team context.
▓ *Analysis, problem solving and creative thinking.* The issue here is a difficult problem and how you solved it; also any other ways in which you could have approached the problem.

Other forms ask about other important abilities such as 'Drive and commitment':

Please give an example of when you set yourself a demanding goal, and detail how you overcame the obstacles to achieve it. (This example should clearly illustrate your determination to complete challenging tasks.)

(British Aerospace)

Notice that at the core of these questions are problem solving, teamwork, interpersonal skills and motivation. When it comes to problem solving, the problem (as long as it is not too light-weight) is not as important as the process. Describe the different ways you thought of solving it, creative or otherwise, and why you picked one method over another. With team-working show that you appreciate how teams work, in terms of benefits and pitfalls; for communication, the importance of tailoring the message to the audience; and with motivation, that you are prepared to give that bit extra when required.

Action steps

▓ When answering, don't just concentrate on what you have done on your course. Illustrate your answers with examples from your employment experience, extracurricular activities or voluntary work.

▓ Don't cram too much into your answers. Describe activities in a logical sequence and make it easy to read. Likewise don't just write one sentence in a space designed to hold a number of paragraphs.

▓ If you get stuck turn back to Chapter 2 and work through the section on Transferable skills. This will help to spark some ideas. Other people can also help to remind you about what you have done: ask your family and friends.

Specific skills

Employers want people with well-developed skills, in particular those concerning communication and IT. Forms will often ask you to list any other languages that you can speak and your level of proficiency (basic, working knowledge or fluent); and about any computer packages or languages that you can use.

Don't claim to be proficient in another language if you only have a very basic ability. Sometimes people are asked to demonstrate their prowess at the interview!

At the very least you should be able to use a word processing package, send and receive e-mails and gather information from the Internet. Don't forget things like statistics, graphics or presentation packages, databases, spreadsheets and any program languages that you know.

If you are a scientist you will be familiar with a range of laboratory and research techniques. If these are relevant include them in this section.

Open fields

Sometimes towards the end of the form you will be asked to respond to an open-ended question. For example, an advertising company might ask you to describe the best advert you have ever seen and why you think it works. Another might ask you about the most difficult thing you have ever done. Some even ask questions like:

If you could change one thing in the world, what would it be?

(Mars)

This type of question often sends applicants into panic. What does the employer want to know? Is this a trick question? The answer is that it is not a trick question (really), just an exercise to see if you can present a convincing argument. There are no right or wrong answers. However, the wise applicant considers the requirements of the job, and his or her personal qualities, and weaves these into the answer.

Action steps

- This is like writing an essay. Plan what you want to say and give your answer structure. Don't just waffle for a couple of hundred words.
- If there are instructions concerning the way in which you are to respond, make sure you follow them. For example, if the question is broken down into a number of sub-questions, ensure that you answer all of them.
- Above all keep your answer(s) relevant and avoid the temptation to be too sensational. It's one thing to provide an interesting response, quite another to convince the employer that you're unstable!

Administrative details

Most forms will ask you to make a declaration about your health and it is in this part that you must reveal any medical condition that could affect your ability to do the work applied for. You may also be asked to disclose details of any criminal convictions. For example, jobs such as teaching fall outside the remit of the Rehabilitation of Offenders Act (1974) and so you must supply any relevant information.

The last part of the form is often a separate section relating to the monitoring of equal opportunities in the workplace. This will need to include your gender, marital status and date of birth, as well as details concerning your ethnic origin and any disability you may have that would produce 'a substantial and long-term adverse effect on your ability to carry out normal day-to-day activities' (Disability Discrimination Act 1995).

Do not get carried away in the health section. This is not asking about minor ailments, only about things that would seriously affect your work performance.

You only need to disclose criminal offences that have led to a conviction. A reprimand for putting a traffic cone on top of a lamp-post is best kept to yourself.

Complete the monitoring section. This sort of information is important in making the selection process as fair as possible, and does not play a part in any decision making.

Referees

Without doubt you will be required to supply the names and addresses of two people who are prepared to give you a reference. You should aim to pick one who is familiar with your academic performance (a head of department, lecturer or tutor) and, ideally, another who can comment on your abilities in a work or non-academic context.

Action steps

- Balance is important. Make sure that you include a referee who can say something about your abilities outside the academic environment. This might be someone you reported to when you had a full-time or part-time job, your manager on a work placement, a sports coach, or the organiser of some form of voluntary activity.
- Never pick a member of your family to act as a referee. Referees are routinely asked what their relationship is with the candidate. Employers will not be impressed if your referee turns out to be a close relative.
- Always ask people in advance if they are prepared to act as a referee. This is not just a question of courtesy, they will need time to decide what to say about you in light of your application.

Declaration

Just like any official form, you will be asked to sign that the information you have supplied is accurate. This might seem like a formality, but if you have included something that is not true, or excluded something that is important, you may face disciplinary action if you are employed on the basis of your 'inaccurate' details.

Action steps

- Think carefully about what you have said. To the best of your knowledge is all the information you have provided honest and accurate?
- If there is something you think you should have said, and there did not seem to be anywhere on the form to say it, attach the details on a separate piece of paper.

▥ Always sign the form! If you don't, your application will be rejected and you will not be considered for the job.

It goes without saying that you should return your form in pristine condition, free from creases, stains and tears. If you are completing a number of forms at the same time, make sure you send them back to the right addresses, and keep photocopies for future reference. Finally:

Action steps

▥ Always make a copy of the form and practise filling it in. Follow the instructions at the top and complete in black ink. If you use a word processor, make sure the form is properly aligned with the printer.

▥ Follow the tips above and make sure that your form contains absolutely no spelling mistakes or grammatical errors. A form full of spelling mistakes will be met with instant rejection.

▥ Don't leave any parts of the form blank. If a section is not relevant, put 'N/A' in the space, or the employer will think you have forgotten to fill it in. Make sure you sign it!

Biodata forms

There is a special application form called a biodata form. This is used to gather detailed biographical information, and also contains a number of questions that are given a rating or score. With these questions you cannot write an answer but have to select one of the options provided.

Examples

What do you consider to be your greatest strength?
(a) Your intelligence (b) Your personality (c) Your skills

Which would you most prefer to do in your spare time?
(a) Learn a new skill (b) Play a team sport (c) Travel to different countries

Which of the following is least important to you in a job:
(a) Direct supervision (b) Working in a team (c) Being paid by results

The fact that there are a restricted number of answers means that questions such as these can be objectively scored; and naturally some things are rated positively and others negatively. The rating system is based on a statistical survey of those factors that predict success amongst the existing graduate workforce. In this way patterns of responses can be used to decide which applicants pass to the next stage. Looking back at the examples, how do you think someone who was suited to a sales job would respond?

Biodata forms are used by about 4 per cent of employers, as they provide a quick way of sifting large numbers of applications. Interestingly they may also be presented over the telephone. A number of organisations, in particular US corporations, use automatic telephone screening systems. These record your personal details and ask you to respond to a series of questions using your telephone keypad. As with paper-based forms, the reason these systems are used is that all applicants are asked the same questions; and they also save the employer a great deal of money as applications can be processed by computer.

There are a growing number of employers who ask you to complete application or biodata forms hosted on the Internet. These are either attached to their own corporate Web sites, and may be the only method of application, or are provided by specialist firms of recruiters or business psychologists. An example of the latter is the Jobsift service (www.jobsift.com) provided by Psychological Solutions Ltd.

Action steps

▓ Biodata forms are easy to identify because they include questions in multiple-choice format. Always carefully consider the requirements of the job before responding.

▓ Most paper forms, and all automatic telephone and computer-based systems, are designed so that contradictory answers can be identified. Make sure that you answer honestly and consistently.

▓ Some 'normal' application forms have separate questionnaires attached. These are more likely to be personality questionnaires (see Chapter 5) than biodata forms. However, the key is still to be honest and consistent.

The curriculum vitae

The curriculum vitae (CV) differs substantially from the application form because you have complete control over the content. This gives you the opportunity to create a powerful personal marketing tool, and to draw an employer's attention to those things you would like to discuss at the interview.

There are a number of different ways in which you can present the information in a CV. However, whatever format you choose, you need to include:

▓ **Personal details.** Give your surname and given names, but indicate the given name you prefer to be known by. Provide your full address and as many other methods of contact as possible (telephone, mobile phone, e-mail, fax etc).

▓ **Educational qualifications.** Concentrate on your most recent qualifications. It is usually quite sufficient to start with your post-16 qualifications and then give details of degree(s) studied, or higher education courses yet to be completed.

▓ **Employment history.** Provide information on any periods of employment in reverse date order, that is, apply the 'most recent, most relevant' rule. This should include your job title or role, responsibilities and achievements.

▓ **Skills.** List any skills you possess that are relevant to your application. For example, you may hold a full UK driving licence, be able to speak another language, or have specific computer skills.

▓ **Interests.** Provide details on two or three interests that help to demonstrate your suitability for the job in question.

▓ **Contact details for referees.** Provide the titles, names and addresses of referees. Employers also find it useful to have telephone numbers.

As you can see, there is not a great deal of difference between the raw information in a CV and the details you are required to provide on an application form, but there should be an enormous difference in the way in which you explain and present the information. To do this you need to reflect in an intelligent way on where you are now, and to project your experience in the most effective form you can.

For many graduates the core of their CV will be their present studies. These should not just be presented as a degree title followed by a tedious list of course units and an anticipated grade. You need to say why you chose a particular course, what you have learnt and the skills you have developed. By the way, if you have already graduated do not miss out your class of degree, otherwise employers will assume you have a Third. In a similar way when you talk about interests it is better to focus on a small number and say what they are, what you get out of them, and the knowledge and/or skill you have gained that may be useful in a work context. For example, if you are a martial arts expert you could describe the way in which it has given you personal discipline and an effective technique for unwinding after a stressful day. As for the work history section, if you have substantial work experience flaunt it! This is what will make you stand out from the crowd. Remember that employers are looking for people who know what it is like to work. Convince them that you have learnt important lessons from your experience. The name of the game is to respond to the employers' needs by providing the right evidence.

As for presentation, you can produce a CV in the same order as the list above or use a skills-based format. The skills approach allows you to link your experience directly to the employer's requirements, to include a personal statement, and crucially to provide details in the most persuasive order. The last point is well worth making, as it is estimated that most managers spend as little as 30 seconds reviewing a CV. In consequence you have to make an impact – fast.

Note that if you include a personal statement it should be no more than 40–50 words in length. You will also need to provide evidence for what you say in the rest of the CV.

Action steps

- ■ A good CV is a short CV, so follow the advice given and try not to cover more than two sides of A4-sized paper.
- ■ Make sure the employer can easily see what you can do. Put things in the most logical and/or persuasive order and use bullet points.
- ■ Check for any gaps in your CV. Employers will view any unaccounted-for periods of time with suspicion.

Electronic CVs

You can present the information in your CV to employers by using the Internet. Some employers will simply ask you to

Figure 4.1 *Example of a skills-based* CV

Alice Hammond
12 Wood Way, Greenfield,
Berkshire SL8 7UK

Telephone: 01624 892233 Mobile: 07768 223400
E-mail: alham@rdx.com

Highly motivated team player with exceptional communication and numerical skills. Proven experience of dealing with customers supported by an understanding of community and social issues. Up-to-date computer ability and a strong aptitude for organisation and training.

Skills profile

- **Communication**
  We routinely give presentations as part of our course work. I have also designed and delivered training sessions to young people (Atlas Flying Camps).
- **Numeracy**
  I have been a fund raiser for a number of organisations and currently keep the accounts for Student Action, the University community volunteer group. On a number of occasions I have run sessions on basic statistics for first year students.
- **Teamwork**
  As a member of the University Gliding Club we work together preparing and launching gliders. In addition I am part of a team of six at Classic Stores, and more recently have been acting Manager when required.
- **Customer awareness**
  I have considerable experience of dealing with the public through my work with Classic Stores. This has involved serving customers, taking orders and dealing with complaints.
- **IT**
  My computer skills include complete familiarity with MS Office (Word, PowerPoint, Excel), MS Outlook Express & Explorer, SPSS for Windows (statistics), and Dream (Web authoring package).
- **Other skills**
  I hold a full UK driving licence and have a working knowledge of French.

Education and qualifications

1998–2001   **Enterprise University, Slough, Berkshire**
BSc (Hons) Biology – Expected grade: 2.1
I enjoy biology because it combines science with nature.
The course covers zoology and botany, and has allowed me
to develop scientific, analytical and statistical skills. My final-
year project involves measuring the ecological impact of a
new road scheme, through laboratory work and a survey of
the views of local residents.

1991–1998   **Arlington Comprehensive, Arlington, Surrey**
Eight GCSE's including English and Mathematics.
A-levels: Biology (A), Chemistry (B) and Physics (C).

Work experience

2000–2001   **Classic Stores, Leverton, Berkshire**
General assistant in a country pursuits store, working on
Saturdays and during all the main vacations.

1999–2000   **Atlas Flying Camps, Merton, W. Yorkshire**
Camp counsellor and assistant organiser to two summer
camps for 15–16-year-olds.

Interests

I am an active member of the University Gliding Club and have gained my
Bronze 'C' badge. This requires 50 solo flights and a number of examinations to be passed. I raise money for the club and enjoy working as part of
the administration team. Other interests include competitive squash playing
and I am a keen member of the Debating Society.

Personal details

Full name: Alice Rosemary Hammond   Age: 21   Nationality: British

Referees

Dr John Newton
Head of Department
School of Biology
Enterprise University
Slough
SL1 2WE
Telephone: 01628 234411
E-mail: newtonj@eu.ac.uk

Mr Allan Roberts
Manager
Classic Stores Ltd
Leverton
Berkshire
RA23 4LP
Telephone: 01234 225577
E-mail: roberts@cdx.co.uk

e-mail your CV, in which case you should send it as a file attachment. Most personnel departments will have the facility to read CVs produced in popular word processing packages such as Microsoft Word. Try to avoid sending your CV as a normal e-mail message as the receiving system may disrupt the formatting; for example, it may force bits of text onto the wrong lines.

The other main electronic route is to post your CV on a graduate recruitment site (see Chapter 3). These will either accept your own format or give you access to a special CV 'writer' so that you can put your details in the right order for their database. Finally you can create your own Web page(s). However, if you decide on this last method you are going to have to think of a good way of getting employers to visit your site; it may not be sufficient just to contact them and provide your Web address.

CV scanning

Sometimes you will need to create a second version of your CV. The reason is that companies are now starting to ask for 'scannable' CVs. When this happens they feed your CV through a scanner linked to a computer. The content is then stored as pure text and can be analysed by a CV tracking system. One of the most popular is called Resumix. This is capable of dealing with thousands of CVs and can be set to 'look' for any combination of keywords. To give you an idea of just how efficient these systems are, a search of 300,000 CVs could be made in only six seconds.

The most important things to get right in this sort of CV are the keywords. The analysis systems are fairly 'smart' and can recognise abbreviations, synonyms and antonyms, and tell the difference between an address and other common forms of formatting, but they do need help. So ensure that you use the right words – there will be plenty of clues in the original advert

– and include alternative keywords where you can. It is also a good idea to put dates before any explanation or description.

Action steps

■ Use lots of nouns. Remember that systems scan for keywords. Also use the correct technical jargon and buzzwords.

■ Don't confuse the scanner. Use lots of space and put important information on separate lines.

■ Keep it clean and do not fold or staple it. Do not include graphics, rules (lines), boxes or any fancy stuff. Print out on white paper only.

Etiquette and covering letters

Let me offer a few words on application etiquette. If you are asked to complete an application form never send a CV, or worse still, attach a CV to an application form with a note saying 'see CV'. Also make absolutely certain that the address you provide on your form or CV is the place you are likely to be resident when the employer replies. If there is any doubt, provide two sets of contact details. Most graduate application forms allow for this eventuality, but you may need to remember to do it if you send a CV. You do not need to provide a stamped and addressed envelope (SAE) for the employers' response unless specifically requested. If you do it will just get in the way when your application is opened and will be thrown straight in the wastepaper basket. Finally, on the subject of etiquette, try not to fold forms or CVs. It will certainly annoy employers if they wish to scan your details into a computer system, and may in any case make your application harder to read.

Whenever you return an application form or submit a CV it

must be accompanied by a covering letter. This is as important as your application, as it is the first document that the employer will read. Indeed some employers seem to pay more attention to the covering letter than the CV. Whatever, a good letter can only increase your chances of getting the job, while a poor one is almost certain to lead to rejection.

The covering letter is designed to draw attention to those aspects of your education and experience that meet the employer's requirements. It must be written in such a way that it looks as if it has been produced especially for the position in question. Never send photocopies, or letters that are typed, with names and addresses written in. All this implies that you need to know something about the organisation to which you are applying. Read the advert and the organisation's literature. You must also make your case in a clear and obvious way: four or five bulleted key points are more than sufficient. And do not merely copy parts of your CV! In addition, mention where you saw the job advertised, if you are sending a CV, and your availability for interview.

Unless otherwise requested you should produce your letter on a word processor or typewriter. It is unusual for employers to request handwritten covering letters, but sometimes they do. When this happens it is possible that your letter will be analysed by a graphologist (handwriting expert). If you have any doubts the best advice is to read a book on graphology before writing your letter. A good introduction is *Teach Yourself Graphology* by Patricia Marne (Hodder and Stoughton, London, 1983).

Action steps

- Ensure that your covering letter is no more than one side of A4 in length. Employers do not read long letters.
- Send your application and letter to the correct person at the right address. If you do not know the person's

correct title or position, contact the organisation and ask.
■ Read your covering letter as if you were an employer. Does it make you want to see this person? If the answer is 'no', write another letter. In fact, keep rewriting until you get it right.

In conclusion, remember that employers are matching your personal details with their current and future job requirements. The easier you can make their task, the better. Thus the more thought you put into your application, the greater your chances of getting to the next stage of the selection process. This means that you will need to spend a considerable time planning and producing CVs, or deciding what to write on application forms. This will certainly run to many hours, if not days.

Finally, to help you on your way, psychologists have found that employers base their first impressions, in order of priority, on the following factors:

■ commitment;
■ motivation;
■ initiative;
■ enthusiasm;
■ interpersonal skills.

When you write about your work experience, construct a personal statement, or compose a covering letter, try to indicate that you have strengths in these areas. And one final word of advice: employers have access to a number of CV checking services. One of the largest vetting organisations, Experian, reports that 50 per cent of major employers say that lying on CVs is a serious problem. The moral is plain: put as positive a construction on your qualifications, skills, achievements and experience as you can, but don't make things up. If you get caught out, especially if you have secured a job, it is often a dismissible offence.

Assessment procedures

The assessment process always starts with the submission of an application form or a CV. What happens next varies between employers, but it will usually include psychometric testing and one or two interviews. Indeed tests are now routinely used by over 80 per cent of major UK employers. In a growing number of cases there will also be one further stage, at a graduate assessment centre. This chapter looks at the different ways in which employers can assess your capabilities, and how you can prepare yourself for the assessment process.

Psychometric tests

Psychometric tests provide a quick and efficient way of measuring abilities and personality. Each test or questionnaire is carefully constructed so that all candidates encounter identical questions under the same controlled conditions. To achieve this level of control they are administered according to a set of detailed instructions, describing how to approach the test, how long there will be to complete the questions, what to do if the instructions are not clear, and so forth. Other parts of the testing process are also standardised, in particular how to mark the answers and the way in which the results can be interpreted.

Tests are designed so that it is possible to compare one person directly with another, or to produce a profile of an individual's strengths and limitations. As such they add objective information which can be used alongside other assessment methods such as the interview. For example, many managers find it difficult to recruit graduates on the basis of the interview alone; they use tests because they provide a fuller picture and allow more informed (and fairer) judgements to be made.

What tests measure

Psychologists classify tests in a number of different ways, but they usually measure either maximum or typical performance. Maximum performance concerns how well an individual can do something, for example use verbal or numerical information; and typical performance how a person is likely to behave in a work setting. From a test perspective the first category includes all types of ability testing, and the second measures of personality, interests, values and other similar characteristics.

Ability tests

It is possible to test for over 50 different abilities. The list includes cognitive abilities such as abstract reasoning; psychomotor abilities like hand–eye coordination; physical abilities relating to speed, stamina and strength; and sensory abilities concerning things like eyesight and hearing. As a result there are something like 4,500 ability tests on the market. However, despite the number of tests available, those used for graduate selection are usually only drawn from the cognitive category, and in particular the abstract, verbal and numerical reasoning tests mentioned in Chapter 2. These can come in a number of different guises, but are often in the form illustrated in Figures 5.1, 5.2 and 5.3.

■ ABSTRACT TEST

Abstract questions consist of a series of shapes in a grid. One of the
shapes from each grid is missing, as indicated by a question mark. The
organisation of shapes within each grid is governed by a fixed rule, and
you have to identify the rule from the shapes provided and then select
which of the six answer options best fits in place of the missing item.

Examples of the Abstract items are shown below. (Please
note they are not to scale.)

Example 1

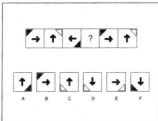

Example 2

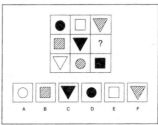

Example 3

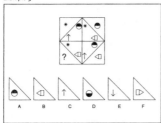

Example 4

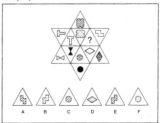

Example 1 The correct answer to this question is D. Going from left to right,
the arrow rotates 90° anticlockwise through each cell. The triangle moves
around the corner of the cells clockwise, and its colour alternates between
black and white.

Example 2 The correct answer to this question is A. Each row and column
contains one of each shape – circle, square or triangle – and each row and
column contains one of each type of shading – white, black or striped.

Example 3 The correct answer to this question is C. The shape in each of the
external cells is the same as those in the nearest corners of the two internal
cells adjacent to it on either side.

Example 4 The correct answer to this question is E. Internal shapes are 90°
clockwise rotations of the external shape in the cells they share an edge with.
The shading of the internal shapes comes from the first external shape
anticlockwise from them.

Figure 5.1   *Abstract reasoning test*

Copyright © NFER-NELSON, 1999. First Graduate Assessment (Test Takers Guide)
reproduced by permission of the publisher, NFER-NELSON Publishing Company Ltd,
Darville House, 2 Oxford Road East, Windsor, Berkshire SL4 1DF, UK. All rights
reserved.

▩ **VERBAL TEST**

The Verbal Test presents you with a passage of information followed by four questions. Each question contains four statements and you have to identify the **two** statements that are true **on the basis of the information given in the passage**. An example of a passage followed by two questions is given below.

The information technology (IT) industry has a very high turnover in personnel. Each year, many companies can expect between 15 and 20 per cent of employees involved with IT to move to other organisations. In some cases, this figure may be as high as 50 per cent. This high turnover rate is very costly to companies, as it takes time and resources to train new employees in the operating procedures and systems of the organisation.

The shortage of well-qualified IT staff is the main reason for the high turnover. In order to attract good staff, organisations now offer high salaries to experienced IT professionals. This encourages people to move jobs frequently in search of higher salaries and new learning opportunities. In order to retain staff, organisations are now realising the value of matching the interests and motivations of potential employees, with those of the wider organisation. By doing this, they are more likely to recruit individuals with a genuine interest in the organisation, who are less likely to leave sooner than expected for reasons such as seeking a higher salary.

Question 1

Which *two* of these statements must be true?

A There is now a surplus of people with IT skills looking for work.

B Higher salaries can encourage IT professionals to move to other organisations.

C Some organisations now examine the motivations of prospective IT employees.

D The IT industry has the highest turnover of personnel of any industry.

Question 2

Which *two* of these statements must be true?

A IT professionals can earn high salaries.

B Some companies lose less than 5 per cent of their IT staff each year.

C High turnover in IT personnel can be costly to companies.

D The longer an IT employee has been with a company, the less likely they are to leave.

For Question 1, the correct answer options are B and C, as both of these are stated in the passage. The passage indicates that there is a shortage of people with good IT skills, so statement A is incorrect and as no information relevant to statement D is provided, the truth of this statement is unknown.

For Question 2, the correct answer options are A and C. Although some companies may lose less than 5 per cent of their IT staff, the passage does not explicitly say this and so B should not be indicated. The passage provides no information relevant to statement D, so the truth of this statement is not known.

Figure 5.2 *Verbal reasoning test*

■ NUMERICAL TEST

The Numerical Test consists of a stem of information followed by four
questions. The stem can present information in a variety of ways, for
example, table, graph, bar chart, text. You have to use the information
from the stem, plus any additional information the question gives you,
to identify which one of the six answer options is correct. An example of
an information stem followed by two questions is given below.

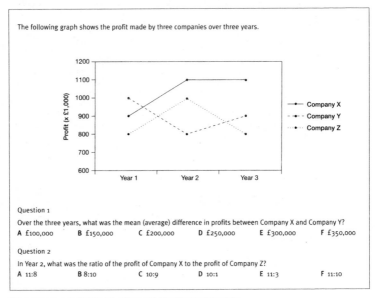

The following graph shows the profit made by three companies over three years.

Question 1
Over the three years, what was the mean (average) difference in profits between Company X and Company Y?
A £100,000   B £150,000   C £200,000   D £250,000   E £300,000   F £350,000

Question 2
In Year 2, what was the ratio of the profit of Company X to the profit of Company Z?
A 11:8   B 8:10   C 10:9   D 10:1   E 11:3   F 11:10

The correct answer to Question 1 is C (£200,000). The difference between the
profits of Companies X and Y is £100,000 in Year 1, £300,000 in Year 2, and
£200,000 in Year 3. To find the mean difference you need to sum these
differences (£600,000) and then divide by the number of years (3).

The correct answer to Question 2 is F (11:10). In Year 2 Company X had profits
of £1,100,000 and Company Z had profits of £1,000,000. The ratio of these
two numbers is 11:10.

Figure 5.3   *Numerical reasoning test*

To give you an idea of what other tests are like, if you apply to be a Royal Air Force (RAF) pilot you will undergo a number of different sorts of testing. In fact the RAF recognises five main 'domains' that are relevant to aircrew selection. These are reasoning, mental speed, spatial awareness, attention and psychomotor ability. Reasoning is best thought of as general intelligence, mental speed as quickness of thought, spatial awareness as knowing which way up you are (!), 'attentional' capability as being able to cope with a high workload under tightly timed conditions, and psychomotor ability as eye–brain–limb coordination.

In practice the five domains are assessed using five computer-based tests:

- **Control of velocity.** In this test you use a joystick to move a pointer left or right to hit targets (small circles) moving down the screen.
- **Instrument comprehension.** This test has a number of parts, but basically you are presented with six aircraft instrument dials and a number of verbal descriptions of the aircraft's orientation. The task is to decide which description best describes what is happening to the aircraft.
- **Sensory motor.** This time you use a joystick and rudder pedals to move a dot so that it is as close as possible to a target in the middle of the screen. During the test the dot actively moves away from the middle.
- **Digit recall.** Sets of numbers of varying length appear on the screen for 5 seconds. As soon as they disappear you have to type the numbers on a keyboard. This is a test of short-term memory.
- **Vigilance.** This is a complex test in which you are presented with a 9 by 9 matrix of numbers on the screen. Stars appear in the cells and you have to cancel them by entering the co-ordinates of the cell, using the keyboard. Occasionally an arrow appears representing

a priority task. The arrow has to be cancelled using a specific key and then by entering the cell co-ordinates.

These are obviously special sorts of test, and involve cognitive and psychomotor abilities. They are also very exacting with a high pass mark, and perhaps make the standard sort of graduate test look quite attractive after all. For some examples of interactive assessments, visit the Royal Air Force Web site at www.raf-careers.com.

Another sort of ability test you should know about is the business learning exercise. These have only been in use for the last few years, and represent a more integrated approach to psychometric assessment. They differ from traditional tests, which usually assess individual abilities, in that they are based on complete problem scenarios. The tests work by leading you through a number of examples that teach you what to do, and then by finding out how you apply what you have learnt in practice.

Large employers such as British Airways and the Halifax use business-learning exercises. They need to select 'fast-track' graduates with a high degree of intellectual capability, who can develop their own concepts for solving problems, rather than rely on fixed patterns or ways of doing things. An example test is Business Decision Analysis from Oxford Psychologists Press, in which you are asked to assume the role of a consultant in a planning consultancy. You have to use various information files to identify the basis on which decisions have been made, and then apply these to new situations. The type of decisions required change as the test progresses. (See Figure 5.4.)

Popular ability tests

Among the most popular graduate selection tests are the *Graduate and Managerial Assessment*, *Critical Reasoning Tests* and *First Graduate Assessment* from ASE; Saville and Holdsworth's *Critical Reasoning Test Battery*, *Advanced*

Figure 5.4 *Example of a business learning exercise*

Instructions

You are a graduate trainee working in a management consultancy firm called Axiom International. Axiom specialises in organisational restructuring and development. As part of an assignment you need to classify three different companies according to a scheme devised by the consultancy.

Axiom classification scheme

Functional organisations have the following characteristics:

▪ Similar activities are grouped in departments or divisions, eg personnel, finance, administration, sales and production.
▪ The business is coordinated through a board of directors, and is controlled on a day-to-day basis by a managing director.
▪ All professional employees have clear career paths. They work with and then manage colleagues with similar qualifications and backgrounds.
▪ Factors such as excessive growth and product or service diversification always put a strain on the structure.

Federal organisations have the following characteristics:

▪ Strategic business units are established for each product, service, consumer group or market.
▪ Accountability is clear at the unit level, as managers or team leaders are easily identified, but is often difficult to assign at higher levels.
▪ Employees experience rapid promotion in successful units. However, poor unit performance typically leads to corporate divestment and redundancy.
▪ Growth leads to the creation of additional units, production facilities or even new businesses.

Task

Look at the company descriptions that follow. In each case decide if the answer is Functional, Federal or Cannot Tell.

1 Treefrog develops and distributes ethical skin care products. It is a small company employing 20 production and development staff in its production facility in South Wales, with a further 15 in administration and sales in its head office in Bristol. Dr John Dare, the Managing Director, was

promoted to his present position eight months ago. He aims to double the size of the business over the next two years. It is anticipated that new staff will be recruited to work in the existing plant in Wales.

2 InGenius is a computer games company. It produces games for many of the major software houses and has specialist teams in three different countries. Each team comprises five programmers and a programmer manager. Currently the firm is having difficulty keeping up with demand. Jez Lucas, the UK Managing Director, admits that the company has had growth pains, and some management problems, but is sure that his policy of promoting from within is a sound approach.

3 Henley Technology operates four self-contained plants. Each produces a different product line for use in the automotive industry. The Group Managing Director, Henry Jones, anticipates strong growth in some areas and plans are in place to open a new brake plant soon. Unfortunately at the same time the commercial hydraulics facility is in danger of closure and 40 people face redundancy. Some may find work in the new plant but overall the workforce will probably remain static at some 200 employees.

Answers. Given the information available the answers are: (1) Functional, (2) Cannot Tell and (3) Federal.

Note: This example has been specially written for this book. It is not part of a previously published business learning exercise.

Managerial Tests, Management and Graduate Item Bank and *Fastrack*; the *Watson Glaser Critical Thinking Appraisal* from The Psychological Corporation; and the *Critical Reasoning Skills Series, Raven's Advanced Progressive Matrices* and *Assessment for Business Learning Exercises* series from Oxford Psychologists Press.

Action steps

▨ Most test publishers produce practice tests. If an employer sends you a practice test make sure that you do it; if not, ask if any are available. You may also be able to obtain practice material from your university or college careers service.

▓ You will find practice tests on a number of Web sites. Try typing 'psychometric' into a search engine or visiting the Web sites of some of the main test publishers, such as www.shlgroup.com/direct or www.ase-solutions.co.uk. Some self-assessment tests are also available on the UK Civil Service Web site at www.selfassess.faststream.gov.uk.

▓ The key to doing better in tests is to develop effective test-taking strategies. The most up-to-date book available is *How to Master Psychometric Tests* (The Times/Kogan Page, 2000).

Personality questionnaires

If you have completed the exercises suggested in Chapter 2 you will realise that there are five important personality dimensions: extroversion, tough-mindedness, anxiety, independence and self-organisation. Typically these are assessed using an untimed personality questionnaire.

The items in questionnaires can be presented in a number of different ways. However, it is usual either to have a choice of responses such as 'Yes', 'No' and '?'(Unsure), or to use a more complex five grade system. Grading systems allow you to indicate if you strongly agree (1) or disagree (5) with a statement, or just agree (2) or disagree (4). As before there is a mid-point (3) that can be used if you are unsure. Some examples are given in Figure 5.5.

Sometimes questionnaires present questions in blocks of four and you have to say which two statements are most like you, and which least like you. In addition they often contain special questions that are designed to detect if you are trying to present yourself in an overly positive way. To put a positive spin on one's personality is a perfectly natural thing to do, but if it is not recognised it does tend to distort the results! Questions of this sort often relate to absolutes, for example, 'Have you ever lost your temper?' You may of course be a very even-tempered

Example 1
1	Are you always early for appointments?	[Yes]	[?]	[No]
2	Do you leave things to the last minute?	[Yes]	[?]	[No]
3	Are you comfortable talking to strangers?	[Yes]	[?]	[No]

Example 2
1	I like my room to be neat and tidy	[1]	[2]	[3]	[4]	[5]
2	I am good at coming up with new ideas	[1]	[2]	[3]	[4]	[5]
3	I like sorting out people's problems	[1]	[2]	[3]	[4]	[5]

Figure 5.5   *Sample personality questionnaires*

person but it is extremely unlikely that you have never lost your temper. In the more sophisticated questionnaires there may even be ways of checking how consistently you have answered. Again the idea is to try to detect those who are deliberately manipulating their answers.

Popular personality questionnaires

There are fewer personality questionnaires than ability tests, but even so there are still over 1,000 to choose from. However, the UK market is dominated by two particular questionnaires. The first is the *Sixteen Personality Factor Questionnaire*™ published by ASE. This is a 'big five' questionnaire, but as the name implies it divides the main personality dimensions into 16 different scales. The second is the *Occupational Personality Questionnaire*®, published by Saville and Holdsworth. The OPQ comprises a family of questionnaires, with the most sophisticated version measuring 32 different aspects of personality. Practically all the UK's top companies use either one of these questionnaires. Other questionnaires that you might encounter are the European edition of the California Psychological Inventory™ from Oxford Psychologists Press, *PIN-POINT* from ASE, and the *15FQ* (fifteen factor questionnaire) from Psytech International.

Action steps

▧ Personality questionnaires are sophisticated ways of assessing personality. Answer honestly and do not try to second-guess the questionnaire designer.

▧ Do not spend too long thinking about each question. While there is not usually a time limit, your first reaction to a question is often the best.

▧ You cannot revise for a personality questionnaire, but it is useful to know how you might fare. Try the questionnaire at www.keirsey.com.

Test administration

As has been mentioned, tests and questionnaires are administered under carefully controlled conditions. Instructions and timings are laid down by test publishers, and the test room is often set out in examination format, that is, rows of tables and chairs facing the front of the room. A typical session lasts between two and three hours and includes two or three timed ability tests (30–40 minutes each) and a personality questionnaire (40–50 minutes).

The test materials are usually in the form of question books and separate answer papers. Answers are recorded in pencil and the answer sheets are then marked with manual 'scoring keys' or automatically scored using an optical mark reading system. Employers may also administer tests on a PC or using a 'palm-top' computer. However, this relies on an organisation having access to enough computers, and so can be difficult to use with large groups of candidates. Additionally some tests can be administered over the Internet. This is an interesting development as it opens up the possibility of 'remote testing' or being able to assess candidates from the comfort of their own homes. However, there are problems, not least ensuring that the right person does the test.

Test interpretation

When someone has completed a series of tests the first step is to mark them to produce 'raw' scores. The raw score is usually the number of questions answered correctly, although sometimes there is a correction to take into account guessing; or with a questionnaire the number of responses that relate to a specific personality dimension. The next step is to compare the results with the correct normative group. This is a large and representative sample of people who have completed the test or questionnaire in the past. For example, with graduates the results will be compared with a sample of UK graduates and managers. The process of comparison allows raw scores to be converted to 'scaled' scores. It is these scaled scores that allow candidates to be directly compared with each other. Scaled scores can be expressed in a number of ways, but the commonest is to describe the results in terms of percentiles. Thus if a candidate scores at the 90th percentile, this is better than 90 per cent of the normative group; or to put it another way, the candidate is in the top 10 per cent.

After test results have been standardised they can be used to select in a number of ways. The three main approaches are 'top-down' and 'bottom-up' selection, or profiling. With top-down selection the top scorers are selected, from the highest downwards, until all the available positions have been filled. The alternative is to use the 'bottom-up' approach, which involves setting a minimum level of performance. This is a point above which candidates have to score if they are to be selected.

Finally, the most sophisticated approach is to profile the results against the requirements for a job. This involves taking account of the relative balance of test results against each other. It is also a way of highlighting the strengths and weaknesses of individual candidates. For example, many managerial jobs require more verbal and numerical ability than diagrammatic ability.

The last part of the interpretation often involves the production of a report. This can be a short set of notes that describe the tests or questionnaires completed, the scores obtained, and the implications in terms of the job, or a comprehensive narrative that explores the results in considerable depth. The latter is typical of personality questionnaires because of the complexity of the subject matter. An extract from the OPQ® is shown in Figure 5.6.

Figure 5.6   *Sample OPQ® narrative*

Note: This is the 'emotion' part of the 'feelings and emotions' section of a manager's report. In a full report there would also be sections relating to 'relationships with people' (influence, sociability, empathy) and 'thinking style' (analysis, creativity and change, structure).

Emotion

Mr Fraser describes himself as relatively free from anxiety or worry. He is likely to find it easy to relax and experiences little tension before important events. He may often be a welcome calming influence on others in tense situations. However, he may also be so relaxed, especially before important occasions, that it could impact upon his motivation and energy levels. Mr Fraser considers himself resilient in the face of criticism, describing himself as unlikely to take offence at insults. Although he has an extremely positive outlook and a resilient nature, he nevertheless tends to feel it is prudent to be suspicious of people. Thus, although his approach may tend to be positive, he is unlikely to be gullible or easily fooled by others. This combination of characteristics could be useful to someone involved in difficult or protracted negotiations.

He describes himself as someone who keeps his emotions and feelings to himself. He may rarely give an indication to others as to how he feels about things, and may appear uninvolved and unemotional. This may be of benefit when his emotions are particularly negative or unconstructive but not when they might otherwise have communicated enthusiasm. His capacity to brush off insults or criticism is likely to be especially powerful when attempting to sell to, or negotiate with others. This may give him the edge in terms of persisting with a sale, but could cause him to come across as thick-skinned and even insensitive to the feedback that others are trying to give him. His willingness to speak out and criticise others when they disagree with his own strong opinions is consistent with his relative insensitivity to criticism or negative comments. He will feel able to shrug off most comments that are passed regarding his perceived stubbornness or inflexibility towards meeting the group consensus. His very positive view is consistent with his reported confidence before important events as well as his calm and relaxed approach more generally. Overall this shows him to be a very positive and relaxed individual, although there is a danger here that he will be seen as overly optimistic or unconcerned about important activities and events. There is an interesting link between his reported clear interest in managing the work of others, and in his perception, however, that they cannot always be trusted. This suggests that others may not find him very empowering, as he is unlikely to express a high degree of confidence in their capabilities and intentions. As well as feeling that others should be viewed with a considerable degree of suspicion, he is likely to make this fairly clear through his tendency to speak his mind openly.

Action steps

- If you are successful in gaining a position you will probably receive some feedback on your test performance. If not, ask the employer if they can tell you how you did.
- Use any feedback to refine your next application. If you have an obvious weakness, try to get some practice in that area. For example, if your numerical ability has let you down, make sure that you understand 'business' maths better, for example, how to interpret charts, diagrams and graphs, calculate percentages and ratios.
- You should also realise that your results may be telling you that you are applying for the wrong sort of jobs. Reassess your target jobs in light of the advice given in Chapter 2.

Interviews

The one thing you can be sure of is that you will not get a job without an interview. The one-to-one interview is the most common, although you should realise that as a graduate you may be interviewed two or three times during a single job application. There is also the possibility that the first interview will be conducted over the telephone. This sort of interview is becoming more common, as it allows employers to screen large numbers of applicants with comparative ease.

The telephone interview should be dealt with in just the same way as any other interview. You will be told when you will be contacted, so make sure that you have access to the telephone and that you can talk without being interrupted. As the interview is being conducted over the telephone you have the luxury of wearing your most comfortable outfit, rather than a new suit, and your CV or application form at hand to check any details. At the end of the interview you will usually be asked if you are still interested in the job; be prepared to answer. The other way in which telephones can be used is as automatic screening systems (see Chapter 4).

The interview format that most people fear is the selection panel. This involves being questioned by more than one interviewer in the same session. The number of interviewers varies but there is often a chairperson, a personnel manager, a technical or professional expert, and sometimes a psychologist. Panel interviews are designed so that an organisation can gather information quickly, and also deal with a number of candidates in turn. Once the panel, or as it sometimes called the board, has finished its deliberations, an employment decision is made. Apart from the fact that panel interviews are often more stressful than one-to-one interviews, interviewers may deliberately put you under extra pressure to see how you react. Indeed it is estimated that nearly two-thirds of graduate interviewers occasionally use 'stress' tactics. If this is the case it is important not to take it to heart, and never lose your temper. It is part of the game, not a personal attack.

Your letter of invitation from the employer should describe the sort of interview you are being asked to attend. If it does not, contact the organisation and find out if you are due to attend a one-to-one (single) interview, be contacted over the telephone, or present your case to a selection panel.

Preparing for interviews

The first thing to do is to make sure that you look the part. What you wear and how you behave is important. You need to buy or borrow the appropriate 'business' clothing. This is the same sort of clothing that people wear in the job. For men this involves wearing a suit, even if an organisation claims to have a relaxed dress code; and for women, image consultants recommend trousers or a skirt of reasonable length and a jacket. Next make sure that you are comfortable in your clothes, especially if they are new. Walk around, shake hands, go up and down stairs. There is nothing worse than attending an interview and feeling as if the clothes hanger is still in your suit.

Interviews make people nervous and tend to magnify repetitive behaviour such as hair twiddling, ear or nose rubbing and hand clasping. If you fidget when you are under stress you will need to do something about it. This does not mean sitting motionless – hand movements, for example, can help you illustrate a point – but you must present yourself in a calm way. The best way to do this is to prepare yourself thoroughly for the questions you will be asked, so that you do not start the interview under stress.

The rule of three

If there is a magic formula for performing well in an interview, it is to take heed of the 'rule of three': know the organisation, know the job, know yourself. This looks like a simple prescription but it is only the best candidates who make sure that they know enough about the organisation, the job and themselves.

Number one: know the organisation

If you have researched an organisation as part of the application process you will already have much of the background information you need. For large organisations, have you:

- ▩ read the organisation's latest annual report?
- ▩ looked at any recruitment brochures?
- ▩ visited their corporate Web site?
- ▩ read any relevant press clippings?

In addition, do you:

- ▩ understand the structure of the organisation?
- ▩ know whether the organisation is growing?
- ▩ know what its aims are for the future?
- ▩ know the names of its main competitors?

This information will help you to answer the classic interview question: 'Why do you want to work for us?' The most powerful response is that you want to work for the organisation because your skills and experience (which include...) match their current and future requirements (which you understand to be...) To fill in the last bit you need to have done some homework. This sort of answer carries far more weight than saying that you want to work for Company X because it's 'the best'.

Number two: know the job

The second part of the rule of three is to understand the job. There will have been some clues in the original advert and you may already know someone doing a similar job, but do you really appreciate what is involved? What does a marketing manager do? Is this different from a sales manager? Clearly the answers are important, as the interviewer will be asking you questions that are designed to see if you have the skills, experience and personality to do the job. There is plenty of information available, and you are well advised to visit your university or college careers service. They will be able to supply you with details and tell you which reference books to read.

A thorough understanding of the job will help you to answer potentially difficult questions such as, 'Where do you see yourself in five years' time?' If you know about the job and understand how it builds into a career, this question becomes easy to answer. Organisation and job savvy also help you to ask intelligent questions at the end of the interview. For example, 'I see that you sometimes sponsor MBA courses. At what stage in my career would this become an option?'

Number three: know yourself

The last part of the rule concerns self-understanding. This is perhaps the vital component as it relates directly to many of the key interview questions. In particular:

- Tell me about yourself.
- What are your greatest strengths?
- What are your limitations?

The interviewer may also tap into this sort of information by asking a series of 'behavioural' questions. For example:

- This job often requires people to work under pressure. Describe a time when you have been under pressure.

You describe an incident. The interviewer then asks a series of follow-up questions such as:

- What were you trying to achieve?

■ What techniques did you use to cope with the situation?
■ Why do you think you were successful (unsuccessful)?
■ What did you learn from the experience?
■ What would you do in a similar situation in the future?

As you can see this is just a more organised way of getting you to concentrate on your capabilities, and relate them directly to a requirement of the job, rather than ask a completely open question such as, 'Can you tell me about yourself?'. By the way, if you get asked open-ended questions you should still relate them back to the job. For the 'Tell me about' question your answer should be a succinct educational and career resumé, with the emphasis on how your CV fits the job.

Whatever the form of the question, if you have analysed yourself by following the advice in Chapter 2, you should be able to answer with authority. The only tricky part is to respond to negatively-phrased questions such as, 'Can you tell me about your limitations?'. With this sort of question never talk about real weaknesses, as these will be interpreted as affecting your ability to do the job. The best thing is to describe a difficult situation that leads back to one of your strengths. For example, you might talk about a group project in which you were the only one who wanted to make any effort. There is obvious potential for irritation and even anger in this situation, as everyone should play their part. However, turn the scenario round and use it as an opportunity to describe your negotiation skills.

The other common interview questions include:

■ Why did you choose course X?
■ What do you think you have gained from your time at university/college?

After studying for a number of years you should know the

answers to both of these questions. Naturally you chose course X because you were interested in X, but also because it would give you an opportunity to develop various specialist skills, such as verbal, numerical and research skills. Likewise, you have developed a broad portfolio of intellectual and social skills from being part of an academic community.

Finally you should be prepared to discuss any additional information you have supplied on your CV or application form, the obvious candidate for a question being your interests or hobbies. Remember that employers want to know about your leisure interests because these say something about how motivated and energetic you are. Talk about two or three activities and describe what you get out of them, and if you're being clever, how the skills you have developed relate to work.

Figure 5.7   *Typical interview questions*

Organisation questions

▒ Why do you want to work for this organisation?
▒ What do you know about us?
▒ Why have you applied for this particular job?
▒ Who else have you applied to? Why?
▒ What do you think a (manager/accountant/advertising executive etc) does?
▒ How do you think you can contribute to this organisation?
▒ Where do you see yourself going in this organisation?
▒ Where do you see yourself in X years' time?

Education questions

▒ Why did you choose to study X?
▒ What other things did you consider? Why?
▒ Which parts of the course are/were the most difficult?
▒ How do/did you cope with them?
▒ Which parts of the course do/did you enjoy the most?
▒ What projects/dissertations have you completed?
▒ What did you learn from them?
▒ What grade of degree do you expect to achieve?
▒ Overall, what do you think you have got out of university/college?

Transferable skill questions

▓ How would you describe your numerical/statistical/IT skills?
▓ Give examples of recent situations requiring these skills.
▓ How would you describe your written/spoken communication skills?
▓ Tell me about a talk/presentation you have given.
▓ How much work do you do in groups?
▓ What do you get out of group working?
▓ What role do you tend to take in group situations?

Work experience questions

▓ Tell me about any part-time/vacation jobs or work placements.
▓ How did you get the job(s)?
▓ What did you have to do?
▓ What did you think you achieved/learnt?
▓ What work-related abilities/skills have you developed?

Disposition questions

▓ How would you describe yourself?
▓ What are your strengths?
▓ What are your limitations?
▓ What areas would you most like to improve? Why?
▓ In what ways do you think you have changed over the last few years?
▓ How would you deal with... (stressful situation, time pressure, personality clash at work, situation requiring flexibility etc)?

Leisure questions

▓ How do you like to relax?
▓ What societies/clubs do you belong to?
▓ What teams/groups do you belong to?
▓ What do you contribute to them?
▓ How do/did you spend your vacations?

Note: Naturally there are variations to all these questions. You should also realise that open-ended questions (what, how, why, where, which) attract follow-up enquiries, depending on your responses. The skilled interviewee anticipates the follow-up by always providing evidence for what he or she is saying when answering the main question. For example: 'I feel that my main strengths are XYZ because...' or 'I am a member of the football team. This helps me to relax and also to develop XYZ team skills...'

Action steps

▓ Some organisations, for example the accountants PriceWaterhouseCoopers, recruit students to help them train their interviewers. You get at least two practice interviews, travel expenses and a small fee. Visit your career service and see what opportunities are available.

▓ Make sure you know the exact location and time of the interview, and leave plenty of time to get there. Take a copy of your CV or completed application form, and don't ever arrive late. Even if it is not your fault it will influence what the interviewer thinks, before you have had a chance to say anything.

▓ Always follow the 'rule of three': know yourself, know the job and know the organisation. This will give you something to say and prime you for the sort of interview questions discussed above.

After the interview

When the interview has finished, ensure that you know what happens next. In practice the interviewer will weigh what you have said against the requirements of the job, and also consider how you have performed compared with the other candidates. Interestingly, research has shown that certain sorts of information tend to carry more weight than others. The order of priority at interview is reckoned to be personality, experience and qualifications. This confirms that first impressions are vital, and that you should assume that the interview has started from the moment you walk into the building. In particular you should recognise that the small-talk that precedes the interview helps the interviewer form a picture of your personality. That being said, the process of comparing candidates takes time, and it is unusual to learn how you have done on the day of the interview. The interview may also be just part of the selection process, with other information being required to make a final decision.

In general you can assume that an interview has gone well if you were able to answer all the questions, if there was a detailed discussion of when you could start, or if the interview lasted longer than usual. Naturally if you are invited to a second interview this is also a good sign. On the minus side if an interview is cut short, and lasts say for only 20 minutes or so, and you are caught out by some of the questions, you are unlikely to proceed any further. However, if you have prepared well you should be able to answer any question you are asked.

Action steps

- ▓ Ask the interviewer how long it will take to make a decision and/or what are the next stages in the selection process.
- ▓ Send a follow-up letter to the interviewer a couple of days after the interview. Thank the organisation for their time and confirm your interest in the job. This will help to keep you in the interviewer's mind.
- ▓ If you think the interview has gone badly make a note (immediately) of those questions that you did not handle well. Think of better answers for the next time you are asked.

Assessment centres

An assessment centre is a selection process that combines the results of interviews and paper-and-pencil assessments with those from a number of job simulation exercises.

Assessment centres are also characterised by the fact that more than one assessor evaluates you. This is important because the involvement of a number of trained assessors

increases the objectivity of the process. Another unique characteristic is that groups of candidates are assessed together. This
allows assessors to observe behaviour in a more natural setting,
and to use interactive assessment tasks. All this makes assessment centres by far the most valid way of assessing candidates
for jobs. As a result they are now widely used, with over half
the medium to large-sized organizations in the UK assessing
candidates using this technique.

The assessment centre is typically run over one or two days,
and often necessitates candidates being accommodated
overnight. For example, about 50 graduates join British
Airways every September. They all attend a one-day assessment
centre that involves an interview, verbal and numerical ability
tests, personality assessment, group discussions and a fact-
finding exercise. The Civil Service Selection Board lasts for two
days and includes a series of tests, group exercises and interviews. It is preceded by a day-long written qualifying test
consisting of four aptitude tests and a questionnaire.

How you are assessed

It is standard practice to use psychometric tests and questionnaires in assessment centres. You can also expect one or two
structured interviews and a number of other assessment tasks.
These tasks are designed to simulate important parts of the job
and include presentations, group exercises, 'in-tray', role play
and analysis exercises. The exercises are picked so that at least
two can be used to gather information on each of the skills or
competencies required to do the job.

Presentations

Assessment centres often include a presentation exercise. These
are usually based on material that is supplied to you in
advance. For example, you may be asked to analyse some

information relating to a business problem and to suggest a solution. Whatever the task, the important elements are the provision of a number of briefing documents, the preparation of a talk, and its delivery to an audience. Needless to say, the preparation and performance are strictly timed. For example, you could be given 30 minutes to prepare a 10-minute talk, with an extra 5 minutes for questions.

A typical scenario might be that you are working in a large department and have been asked to gather information on the way in which customer records are processed. You are to prepare a talk that describes the existing system and ways of making it more efficient.

When you deliver a presentation you are rated on content (do you present information in a logical sequence?); argument (is your case convincing?); delivery (is your presentation well paced?); and response (can you cope with questions?).

Presentations are used to assess spoken communication ability. They can also provide valuable information on attention to detail, problem analysis, judgement, decisiveness and personal impact.

Action steps

- ▓ If you have had only a little experience of public speaking, you need to practise. If you are at university or college, volunteer to present a paper in a seminar, contribute to a student meeting or give a talk in a school.
- ▓ The trick to getting a good mark in a presentation exercise is not just being able to talk clearly; you must be able to write the presentation. Practise by preparing notes for a short talk on a subject with which you are unfamiliar.
- ▓ If the thought of giving a talk fills you with horror, you need to develop ways of coping with your anxiety. The

best way is to practise and also to find ways of relaxing. Look in the library for books on relaxation techniques, meditation and visualisation.

Group exercises

There are many different forms of group exercise. However, all of them involve 'debating' a prepared topic or the group working on a given problem. For example, in 'leaderless discussion groups' candidates are all given the same brief and asked to discuss a particular work issue, or debate a controversial topic such as human cloning or how to avoid famine in the Third World. As the discussion is leaderless, the aim is to discover how the group members organise the discussion and interact with each other. Thus you are monitored on the nature and pattern of your contributions. For example, are you leading, asking questions, suggesting solutions, supporting others or summarising the debate?

Leaderless group discussions usually take about an hour, and are used to gather information on spoken communication, listening, persuasiveness, teamwork, initiative and flexibility.

More complex group discussions are based on assigned roles and a problem scenario in which group members have competing interests. For example, the members of the group may be asked to assume the roles of divisional managers in a particular company. Your role is then to negotiate with the others and get them to allocate funds to your particular project. Sometimes the task may be complicated by the fact that whatever decisions are made must be in the best interests of the company as a whole.

In assigned-role group discussions there will always be winners and losers. However, being a loser does not mean that you will get a low mark: the structure and quality of your arguments are more important. Indeed in some scenarios you will receive extra credit for realising that you should be supporting another candidate.

Assigned-role group discussions are highly structured, with specific times allocated for preparation and discussion. So you will have 30 minutes to read the briefing documents and prepare a case, and 60 minutes for the main discussion. Within the discussion you will be allocated a fixed time, say 10 minutes, to present your case without interruption.

This sort of exercise is used to assess communication and persuasiveness skills, as well as qualities like interpersonal sensitivity and organizational ability.

Action steps

- ▓ As with presentation exercises, you must be able quickly to assess unfamiliar information and prepare a case. Practise, practise, practise!
- ▓ The task is centred on persuasion and debate. Think back to those occasions when you have got what you wanted, against the odds. What verbal techniques did you use? How could you apply them in this situation?
- ▓ The sorts of skill that are assessed in group exercises can be developed in any sort of team or group. Try joining a committee, volunteering to be a club secretary, working in the Students' Union or organising a sports team.

In-tray exercises

The in-tray exercise is designed to assess the paper-based aspects of a job. The task is to manage an in-tray containing up to 30 items, typical of the position in question. Thus the in-tray contains information in a variety of forms that must be dealt with in a fixed period of time. The items usually include letters, faxes, reports, computer print-outs, telephone messages, e-mails and so on. You may also have documents relating to the structure of the organisation, so that decisions can be delegated if appropriate.

The task is to sort through the material, produce a list of what needs to be done in order of priority, and then action each item. This may involve writing a memo, letter or fax to a named person, deciding to make a phone call (and indicating what you would say), or ignoring low-priority information. Sometimes as the in-tray exercise progresses, work is collected and new items are delivered. In this situation you need to reassess all the items remaining in the in-tray!

A typical scenario is that you have just taken over a new job. Your predecessor has left a full in-tray. You have two hours to clear the in-tray before your first meeting. At the meeting (15 to 20 minutes) you will be asked to explain how a number of projects, based on the items in the in-tray, are progressing. Note that this type of exercise is generally a paper-and-pencil task, but it is possible to be given entirely computer-based 'e-basket' assessments.

In-tray exercises provide information on written communication, planning, problem analysis, judgement and delegation. If they are combined with a verbal debriefing, they can also be used to assess spoken communication, independence and initiative.

Action steps

▓ If you have had some substantial work experience you will be much better prepared for this sort of exercise. If nothing else, now may be the time to help out in an office with some routine administrative tasks.

▓ In-trays are about organising and prioritising. Think about how you organise your everyday life and the ways in which you cope with unforeseen circumstances. How can your natural organising ability be applied to this sort of exercise?

▓ It may sound obvious but if you don't know what a memo looks like, a business report or a print-out of a computer spreadsheet, find some to examine. Any office will contain plenty of examples.

Other exercises

Assessment centres often include role plays that are designed to simulate the face-to-face aspects of a job. For example, you may be asked to deal with a (trained) manager playing the part of a dissatisfied customer or client. Exercises such as these are good ways of assessing customer service, listening and interpersonal sensitivity. If a scenario requires you to deal with a subordinate, possibly as a result of a breach of discipline, it can also provide information on people management and leadership capabilities.

Other highly interactive and practical exercises may take place outdoors. These are often centred on construction tasks, for example building a bridge or other structure out of a limited supply of materials, and can only be completed by candidates cooperating with each other. As with discussion groups the aim is to determine what sorts of role people naturally assume. Who takes the lead? Who designs the bridge? Who actually builds it? Who comes to the fore when things go wrong?

Finally, in many fast-track assessment centres analysis or fact-finding exercises are used. These involve you analysing various sorts of data, both quantitative and qualitative, in order to produce a written report. For example, you may be given information on the pros and cons of relocating a business. Your task is to identify the key issues and make an appropriate recommendation.

Analysis-type exercises generate information on written communication, planning, detail consciousness, judgement and decisiveness. Commercial awareness and numerical ability can also often be assessed.

Action steps

- ▨ To practise for role plays, try the 'angry customer' scenario with a friend. To get a good score in the real thing you will need to respond appropriately, in a timely manner. If you tend to be a bit tongue-tied, the more practice you get the better.
- ▨ Construction tasks do not necessarily favour those with latent engineering talents. Candidates often fail to complete tasks because they spend too long planning and insufficient time building, or vice versa. Seek out opportunities to take part in practical projects and work on the role of project manager: the person who makes sure that the job gets done properly, on time!
- ▨ Analysis tasks are intellectual exercises. If you are skilled at writing critically reasoned essays (rather than just describing facts) you should not encounter any problems. Those who are a bit rusty in this area will need to practise.

The moment of truth

The results from tests, interviews and assessment centre exercises are matched in a systematic way against the requirements of the job. Obviously information may be provided by a number of methods, but some will be better than others. For example, individual problem solving can be assessed through interviews and group exercises, but it is likely that analysis and in-tray exercises will provide better information. In consequence, some results are given more weight than others. This allows information to be collated objectively, and avoids too much attention being given to exercises that may be relatively poor indicators of particular abilities.

The score for each participant in an assessment centre is considered along with the notes made by the assessors. This takes place in a so-called 'wash-up' meeting at which all the assessors try to arrive at a unanimous decision on the candidate or candidates that will be offered jobs. Such meetings can take a number of hours; it will also be a number of days before you are told whether you have been successful or not.

There are a limited number of books on assessment centres, and even fewer written from the point of view of the participant. Try *How to Succeed at Assessment Centres* (Trotman Publishing, Richmond, 1995); or the classic (and readable) volume for assessment centre designers, Charles Woodruffe's *Development and Assessment Centres – Third Edition* (CIPD, London, 2000). After all, there is nothing more effective than knowing the thinking behind the exercises you are likely to have to complete!

Starting work

Congratulations on your new job! If you have won a place on a graduate training programme, you are one of a lucky 18,000 graduates who start on company schemes each year. At a financial level, if you have a good degree and have been recruited by a top FTSE company you may also have secured an attractive package including share options, free loans and other benefits. Indeed, as part of your 'golden hello' you may even have secured a signing-on bonus of £10,000 or so, bringing your starting salary to £30,000. However, even if you get a more moderate salary you will still enjoy an income that is higher than your non-graduate contemporaries. This chapter looks at what will happen during the first few years of your employment, in particular at development programmes and appraisal systems. Our first stop is the employment contract.

Employment contracts

To become a new employee you will need to have accepted a formal offer of employment. This will have come in the form of a written offer before you started your job, and will include details on the organisation, the date of the offer, your job title, salary, period of notice and start date. There may also be additional information on hours of work, holidays and other aspects of the employment package. For some, it will be clear that the offer is contingent on achieving a certain degree grade, satisfactory references or passing a medical.

The other part of the engagement process is your letter of acceptance. This is an important communication as it forms part of your employment contract. In this you will have accepted and confirmed the date of the offer, your job title and the starting date.

Action steps

- ■ A verbal offer isn't worth the paper it's written on! Do not start a job until you have an official letter, signed by someone in authority, offering you the job.
- ■ Make sure you understand any conditions attached to the offer. For example, if you are to be employed initially for a probationary period, get the details in writing.
- ■ Keep copies of all correspondence, including your letter of acceptance. Remember this forms part of a legal contract between you and the employee; if things go wrong you may need to provide copies.

Terms and conditions

In addition to any offer letter, you are legally entitled to written particulars of the main terms and conditions of employment within two months of starting work. This will reiterate some of the details you should already know, but will include other information as well. The 'official' contract must contain, or refer to the following particulars:

- ■ your name and the name of the employer;

- your job title;
- starting date;
- commencement of continuous service;
- pay scale;
- intervals at which pay is credited (usually monthly);
- hours of work and usual working hours;
- holiday entitlement;
- entitlement to holiday pay;
- provision of sick pay;
- pension details, if applicable;
- length of notice you (and the employer) are required to give if employment is terminated;
- the disciplinary rules that apply (eg regarding drug taking, theft, antisocial behaviour and misuse of company facilities and equipment);
- who to apply to if you are dissatisfied with any disciplinary action;
- details of the disciplinary procedure (eg number of verbal and written warnings);
- who to apply to if you have any grievance relating to your employment;
- information on the company's training policy (in firms employing more than 20).

There will usually also be details on other benefits, such as those relating to maternity, as well as statements on redundancy procedures and confidentiality. The latter will refer to the return of company equipment and paperwork on termination of employment, and may exclude you from contacting a company's clients or customers for a fixed period after you have left. Often you will receive a staff handbook which gives further information in all these areas, and may in addition include a brief history of the organisation.

Action steps

- If you have not received a full written contract within two months of starting work, contact the appropriate person, usually the personnel or HR manager, and ask when you can expect to receive one.
- Employment contracts are intensely boring documents. However, read it carefully and check that the details correspond with your original offer letter.
- Do not sign your contract until the details are correct.
- As part of your 'starter-pack' you should also receive details on induction procedures and training programmes. Again, make sure that you have the details before proceeding.

Induction and development

As part of the induction process you will be introduced to your boss and work colleagues, shown your desk and given a tour of the premises. You will be issued with numerous manuals and associated paperwork. In large organisations you will be treated to introductory presentations and films. Finally you will be issued with your work 'tools', such as a laptop computer, mobile telephone and company car.

Starting a new job is always confusing. Despite the fact that you may have a skilled and understanding boss, your early days will be spent getting to grips with procedures and learning how to deal with the organisation's culture. During this 'honeymoon' period you and the employer need to make sure that the job is right for you, and even if you think you are in the right job, you still need to avoid being dismissed at the end of your probationary period! Advice on this tricky topic is given at the end of the chapter.

Employers know that it is difficult to retain graduates for any length of time. In fact most organisations are lucky if they have half their graduate recruits five years after they join. This is an expensive problem to have, and because 'good' graduates are in short supply, employers invest considerable energy in providing the right sort of motivational and development opportunities.

The magnificent seven

As a graduate you should expect your employment experience to meet seven important criteria:

- **The delivery of promises.** It seems obvious, but you should get what you were promised in terms of type of work and opportunities for development and progression. Unfortunately the advert that attracted you in the first place may not be a true reflection of the job you find yourself doing. This mismatch often leads to dissatisfaction and lack of commitment.
  Problems? If you find that your new job does not live up to its billing you can quite legitimately ask the employer why they are not keeping to their part of the bargain.
- **The right work for you.** You will have been through a rigorous selection procedure, and should expect challenging and stimulating work that uses your abilities to the full. There will of course be routine tasks to do, but in general the work that you are given should be of a 'graduate' level. In particular, you should expect to be given early responsibility for projects, and possibly other employees.
  Problems? If there seems to be a gap between what the job demands and your capabilities, ask for the job to be reviewed.
- **High-quality development.** To be able to do your job well you will require both on and off the job training.

Indeed you should have a full training programme designed for you (see the section that follows). This must be of a suitable quality and be appropriate to your job. It is also fair to say that it should be a mandatory part of your employment, and that your day-to-day work should be structured so that you have time to study.

Problems? A common problem is for managers to prevent attendance on training courses because of work pressures. If this happens, enlist the help of the training and development manager.

▓ **Good career management.** You will need help and support from your employer concerning career management. This should include general careers advice, guidance on the career options available in the organisation, and help with securing suitable placements. Despite talk of 'portfolio' careers and the emphasis placed on managing your own career, you should not be left to fend for yourself.

Problems? You should expect to have suitable career counselling throughout your training programme, and especially towards the end when you are considering what specialist management area to enter. Make sure you ask if guidance does not appear to be forthcoming.

▓ **Work–life balance.** As a new graduate you will be expected to commit yourself to the work of the organisation. This may require long working hours and further periods of study, especially if you wish to gain a professional qualification. However, it is unreasonable for an employer to demand protracted periods of 'round-the-clock' working or to impose conditions that damage family life or personal relationships.

Problems? Many employers are becoming more enlightened and actually encourage new employees to seek a proper balance between work and home life. If you feel under unreasonable pressure you must speak up, otherwise you will find yourself off work due to tiredness and stress.

▦ **Appropriate career progression.** Graduates are recruited because employers believe they will make the senior managers of the future. In consequence, while your rise through the ranks may not be meteoric, you should, as long as you do your job well, anticipate some form of promotion.

Problems? Graduates often report that they feel stuck in a particular role or position. Make sure that you apply for internal promotions as they arise, and if you feel you have been bypassed unfairly, consult the personnel manager.

▦ **Management support.** The key player in your relationship with the organisation is your immediate line manager. He or she is there to make sure that you understand what to do and have the resources to do your job properly. Your line manager should also be a good role model, and be practically involved in your training and development. As you will see later in this chapter, your manager will also be responsible for appraising your progress.

Problems? The hardest problem to deal with is when you have a personality clash with your manager. However, remember that you do have rights in the organisation, and if things get difficult you will have a documented route through which you can address any grievances (see your employment contract).

Not all employers are perfect, and the seven factors mentioned might not all be evident in your job. But in the long run it is for you to decide if you are getting what you want out of your employment, and if not, what to do about it. In particular you should pay attention to the development programme, as this will help you to increase your range of transferable skills. Such skills will be vital to gaining promotion within the organisation, and also to getting another job with a different employer should you choose to leave.

Development programmes

Graduate development programmes are designed to enable you to realise your full potential. When you join an organisation you will generally be expected to develop your skills and experience by moving between divisions, management functions and even markets. A full training programme will include an induction process (as already mentioned), skills training, work towards professional qualifications and a periodic process of review and appraisal. An example programme is briefly described in Figure 6.1.

Action steps

- Check that your development programme gives you exposure to different management functions.
- Ensure that the programme contains basic skills modules and a thorough introduction to the role of the manager.
- Confirm that you will be able to continue your development and study for a professional qualification.

Mentoring

An important element of the United Biscuits programme, and many other graduate development schemes, is mentoring. Indeed in the UK about 30 per cent of all medium to large-sized firms have some form of mentoring scheme. Such schemes are developmental in nature and typically take place 'offline': that is, the relationship is not usually between a manager and his or her graduate trainee, but with a different or more senior manager.

Figure 6.1 *United Biscuits graduate development programme*

United Biscuits

Induction and mentoring

Over the first week new graduates attend a residential introduction to United Biscuits (UB). This focuses on the development programme and the UB career planning process. The next step is to move straight into a functional role, but to attend, over a period of six to nine months, a series of modules introducing other functions and parts of the business. The modules are based on particular work projects. At the beginning of the process graduates are also introduced to a senior manager who will act as their mentor.

Understanding Business programme

This is a professional programme run and accredited by Henley Management Centre. It is split into two parts: Essentials and the Diploma programme. The Essentials programme starts after about 12 months and focuses on the behaviours that make an effective manager and a personal development plan. There are five modules that are taken at intervals of two to three months. Each module lasts two to three days.

The Diploma programme allows graduates to specialise in the UB business area that interests them the most. It comprises residential modules that span two or more years and periods of home study. There are reports to prepare and examinations to take. At the end of the course, if a graduate has passed all the modules and produced a major project report, a Diploma in Management is awarded.

Functional development

For each function within UB there are ongoing development programmes. External trainers provide the programmes, for example the CIPD for HR graduates and CIMA for finance graduates. There are also specialist UB programmes such as the World Class Customer Management Programme.

The United Biscuits scheme is a good example of a high-quality professional training programme. All the major blue chip employers run similar schemes.

A mentoring relationship is confidential. It is for both parties to agree how it is to work and to commit time to regular meetings. In some ways it is similar to having a personal tutor at university or college, but this time the 'tutor' is there to introduce you to the business culture. Often the mentor will be significantly older than the graduate trainee; an age gap of 10 to 15 years is not unusual. Thus a new graduate will often be placed with a mentor in their mid-thirties or early forties.

The benefits of being mentored include:

▓ an individual introduction to your new job;
▓ the confidence of having someone batting on your side;
▓ tailored careers advice and possible advancement;
▓ expert managerial guidance.

The last point is important because your mentor will be able to provide useful insights into how the management process operates, and the unwritten rules that influence how the organization operates. Indeed an understanding of the unwritten rules, those that never appear in any manual or handbook, is often the key to success. For example, what are the informal lines of communication within the organisation?

Action steps

▓ Mentoring schemes only work if both sides invest sufficient energy in the process. Make sure you thoroughly understand the mechanics, and what you will be required to do.
▓ Be proactive in the relationship and ask your mentor what you can do to advance in the organisation. Unlike the US, in the UK mentors are not there to help you get promoted, but they do know what it takes. Make sure that you listen!

▧ If you join an organisation that does not have a mentoring scheme, ask if there is a senior manager you can use as an unofficial mentor or sounding-board. It is flattering to be asked to act as a mentor, so there should not be a problem with you adopting your own.

Appraisals

From time to time during your training period, and indeed throughout your career, you will be required to attend appraisals. These are reviews that take place between you and your manager, which provide an opportunity to discuss your performance. The idea behind appraisals is actually very simple: they are designed to ensure that you know exactly what your job involves, how you have done, and how you will know if you have performed well enough.

The appraisal usually takes the form of an interview, with the focus on achievements and progress, leading to a plan of action for the forthcoming period. Your manager will have an up-to-date description of your job and notes on how you have performed on different projects. During the interview the manager will analyse the reasons you have been successful or not, decide where to give praise, and how to deal with under-performance. There will also be a discussion of your personal objectives for the forthcoming year, and how you feel that the organisation can help you achieve them.

Some organizations will allow you to prepare formally for appraisals and to complete a comprehensive self-appraisal questionnaire that will form the basis of the discussion.

Whatever the preparation, you will be invited to consider your own performance, and important matters will then be analysed jointly. Your manager will make sure that the discussion is based on facts and not opinions, and on your performance rather than your personality. This is done by concentrating on real work events, and by leading you through a series of questions that relate to the particular situation. For example:

- How did you plan for project X?
- Who worked with you?
- How did you work together?
- What did you do?
- How did you allocate responsibilities?
- What was the outcome?
- Why were you successful/unsuccessful?
- What did you learn about yourself?
- What did you learn about working with others?
- What would you do differently in the future?

Of course your manager will already know the answer to some of these questions, but the point is to discover how you perceive things. Importantly, you must be honest in your analysis and realise that in those situations where things did not go according to plan, the manager's job is not to criticise or to attribute blame. This sort of feedback, if deserved, should have been delivered at the time. The manager's job is to find ways of moving on and making sure that you are properly equipped for similar situations in the future. This is achieved by agreeing honest, measurable and realistic objectives. Such objectives will usually include the provision of appropriate training, and successful performance may also be linked to an increase in salary or a bonus.

360-degree feedback

As mentioned, the appraisal process may include question-naires. In some organisations this will take the form of '360-degree' feedback, a relatively new technique but one that is becoming increasingly popular. This type of appraisal takes the form of a questionnaire that is issued to trainees and their colleagues, managers, and in some instances customers or clients. It provides an all-round view of an individual and provides a powerful technique for identifying development needs and improving performance.

An example of a 360-degree questionnaire is Skillscope®, distributed in the UK by Oxford Psychologists Press. This is designed for junior managers and is based upon managerial roles and the skills required to perform them. It is a 98-item questionnaire that looks at 15 different skills clusters, with at least six questionnaires being completed for each person! The questionnaire assesses:

▩ obtaining and making sense of information;
▩ communicating information and ideas;
▩ taking action, making decisions;
▩ risk-taking, innovation;
▩ energy, drive, ambition;
▩ relationships;
▩ influencing, leadership, power;
▩ openness to influence, flexibility;
▩ administration/organisational ability;
▩ managing conflict, negotiation;
▩ time management;
▩ selecting, developing people;
▩ knowledge of job, business;
▩ coping with pressure, adversity, integrity;
▩ self-management, self-insight, self-development.

'Skillscope' is a registered trademark of the Center for Creative Leadership, Greensboro, NC 27438-6300, USA.

Action steps

▩ You must prepare for an appraisal. Make detailed notes on how you have met your objectives, both in business and personal terms. If you have information from questionnaires at your disposal, carefully consider what it means.

▓ Be prepared to comment critically on your own performance and suggest ways of improving it in the future. For example, you could identify extra training or career development opportunities.

▓ Be ready to discuss any pressing issues concerning the nature of your work and your long-term prospects. In some appraisals, especially if you have performed exceptionally well, there may be scope to discuss promotion or increased pay.

Development centres

During your first few years in an organisation you may be invited to take part in a development centre (DC). This is a development 'event' which takes place away from the workplace, in which you and a small number of colleagues will complete a range of job-related exercises. These are similar to the sorts of exercise used in assessment centres (see Chapter 5) and include psychometric tests, structured interviews, problem-solving tasks and group exercises. Specially trained managers closely observe all the participants.

In contrast to an assessment centre, a DC is not concerned with selecting people for jobs. Rather, the information generated is used in conjunction with appraisal ratings, on-the-job performance and an individual's career aspirations, to produce a development report. This may be concerned solely with personal development, or be used to introduce a competency framework to prepare participants for higher-level jobs. Competencies are just business-related transferable skills, or those things that have been shown to distinguish good performers from the rest.

The report is written after the centre, although some parts will have been discussed during the assessment period, and summarises the developmental evidence gathered through the exercises. Participants gain access to their own reports about two or three weeks after the DC, at which time they also receive detailed feedback from one of the observers. In addition they will have had an opportunity to comment on the DC using feedback forms, and to express personal views which will have been taken into account during the preparation of each report. In most DCs, reports remain confidential and form part of a participant's personnel file. However, depending on the outcome of the DC, line managers or mentors will usually need to be aware of the comments as they will be involved in drawing up development plans. Such plans will usually incorporate a range of different training options, details on individual targets, and how progress will be evaluated. A development report usually remains valid for between 18 and 24 months.

To illustrate the way in which information is used, the results of personality questionnaires are often discussed candidly with individuals during the course of the DC. For example, 'emotional intelligence' (EI) questionnaires are used to shed light on the extent to which we are in tune with our feelings and emotions, and the ways in which we manage our relationships with other people. An excerpt from the EI report for the *Occupational Personality Questionnaire*™ is reproduced in Figure 6.2.

Staying employed

Development programmes excepted, when you join an organisation you will often be placed on probation. During this period you must do everything you can to fit in to the organisation, and to shine. This is not easy, but the following tips may help you to keep your feet under the desk.

Figure 6.2 *Emotional intelligence (EI) report for the Occupational Personality Questionnaire*

Managing feelings

Feelings and Emotions: Your scores show an interesting contrast between the emotions your experience internally and the feelings that you share externally with others. While, on the one hand, you describe yourself as someone who is generally calm and relaxed, you also describe yourself as someone who is guarded in the feelings that you share with others, perhaps preferring to be seen as a calm realist rather than a wishful optimist.

■ While you may see being calm and rational as a strength, not expressing or sharing the excitement and enthusiasm of others may also be seen as lacking warmth or indifference. Consider a recent situation in which you could have shown more buy-in to an idea, project or event through expressing greater interest and enthusiasm to others.

■ Your ability to cope when things go wrong or to stay calm when emotions are running high may be a strength that is hidden from others. Sharing your strength with others will help to close the distance that others may feel between you and them. It may also help them to discover the emotional capacities that you bring to resolving problems and issues.

Personal Insight: Your scores suggest that you are someone with the capacity to understand patterns in your own thoughts and actions, and that you are someone who is capable of deep personal insights into your own emotions and those of others. While you may prize the suggestions and feedback of others regarding your behaviour, there may also be occasions when you need time to appreciate the impact of your actions on other people.

■ What are the most significant insights that you have had recently into your own thoughts and feelings, and into what motivates you to act in the ways that you do? Has your sense of yourself changed recently and, if so, why? How does your view of yourself today match the role that you have or that you want to undertake next?

■ Are there people that you have observed recently from whom you feel that you could learn in terms of their approach to problems and in the way they behave with others? What have you observed that you feel would enable you to develop a better understanding of yourself, and how would you incorporate that understanding in your everyday work?

Managing relationships

Empathy: Your scores suggest a strong need for independence and that you may feel that involving others in making decisions only serves to complicate matters rather than get things done. This need for independence may express itself to others as a general disinterest in them, or as a preference for keeping people at a distance in order to avoid getting involved in the thoughts and feelings of other people.

■ While retaining your independence may be important to you, consider how this may cut you off from information that others have about what is going on and what the future may hold. If they consider you to be disinterested and unconcerned about what they know and what they feel, then they will not feel obliged to share their knowledge and understanding with you. As well as you consulting them, this may assist you to achieve your objectives more easily and with greater satisfaction than might at first be obvious to you. Active listening to others and offering them opportunities to contribute to conversations and discussions is something that will strengthen the positive view others will have of you as a team member and a potential mentor.
■ Refer to your score under Personal Insight. If this is low, then this suggests a potential blind spot in that the true impact you have on other people may be something that is hidden from your view. If others feel a strong sense of distance from you, then they are unlikely to share thoughts and feelings with you or to provide you with feedback on your strengths and development needs.

Social ease: Your scores suggest that you are someone who enjoys the company of other people and who develops strong attachments to others. You are likely to enjoy being the centre of a discussion or conversation and be relaxed in the company of others.

■ Your scores suggest that you are someone who is likely to make a positive impact on other people when engaging in a group at work or socially. While you are also likely to make an impact in such situations, the nature of that impact is also indicated by your Personal Insight and Empathy scores.
■ If your Empathy score is low, others may find your natural confidence and exuberance very powerful, and may feel that, while you are sharing your own thoughts and feelings with them, you are not listening or attending to their thoughts and feelings. If your Personal Insight score is also low, then you may not be aware of this effect on others. If both your Empathy and Personal Insight scores are low, then you should consider how to adjust your style and approach with others to give them a more positive sense of their interaction with you. For example, by encouraging them to contribute and participate, and by giving them an active sense of your presence by the way you signal that you are listening to them.

■ **Actively introduce yourself.** You may be tempted to hide until you feel you have something to offer, but you must 'join' the organisation. This means actively introducing yourself to colleagues, managers other than your immediate boss, and to anybody else whom you think is influential. Most people are dismissed because the organisation thinks they do not fit the corporate culture.

■ **Demonstrate market knowledge.** It is important to know what the competition is doing. Join the appropriate professional organisation, read the trade press and keep up to date with the newspapers. Don't miss opportunities to demonstrate to others that you have your finger on the pulse.

■ **Give more than you are asked for.** This does not necessarily mean working day and night; rather, it involves treating everyone in the organisation as if they were a customer. Make sure you find out what you can do to help, and act on requests with polite efficiency. In short, make a point of always giving that little bit extra.

■ **Seek feedback on your performance.** It is good to know how you are doing; psychologically it also sends a powerful message to others if you ask them to assess your progress. In some organisations you will be assessed automatically, but in others you will have to make the running. Ask for a meeting with your boss after about six weeks have elapsed.

■ **Adopt and develop a project.** As a newcomer you will be given various routine tasks to complete. Look on these as opportunities to stamp your personality on your work, and as a way of showing others that you add value to the organisation. Look on all tasks, however small, as an opportunity to demonstrate your worth.

■ **Become a recognised team player.** You need to strike a

balance between individual and group activity. Remember that organisations actively look for good team players, so make sure you do not miss any opportunity to work and collaborate with others. It also does no harm to volunteer to take the lead on a (straightforward) project early in your career. Ask if you can be in charge of a project.

Finale

For many, securing a place on a graduate training programme is the start of a long and successful career. For others, that brilliant job turns out not to be so good after all. The hard sell of the graduate recruitment advert does not live up to expectations, and the promised career turns out to be just another job. If you find yourself in this position ask for help: all graduates need guidance and encouragement from their employers in order to manage their careers. Not only that, but there is an extremely powerful economic reason for employers to develop their graduate talent.

Research has shown that the top 10 per cent of employers retain 80 per cent of their graduates over five years, whereas the bottom 10 per cent only hang on to 20 per cent. This is an enormous gap, and with each graduate costing about £200,000 in recruitment, salary and training costs over the same period, it knocks a big hole in any organisation's budget. In fact, given the average intake of graduates, the difference between the top and bottom amounts to some £3,000,000.

An employer would be mad to lose you! However, if you are genuinely being treated like Cinderella – held back and taken for granted – look for another job. It's your career, your life and your future.

References

In addition to those sources identified in the text, statistics are reported from the following publications:

Chapter 1

Arberry Pink (1999) *Kaleidoscope: Top Careers for Ethnic Minority Graduates*, Arberry Pink, London

Association of Graduate Recruiters (AGR) (2000) *AGR Graduate Salaries and Vacancies Survey*, AGR, Warwick

Association of Graduate Careers Advisory Services (AGCAS) (2000) *Attitudes and Voices*, AGCAS, Sheffield

Department for Education and Employment (DfEE) (1999) *Helping Graduates into Employment*, DfEE Skills and Enterprise Briefing, Issue 1/99, DfEE, London

DfEE (2000) *The Changing Graduate Labour Market*, DfEE Skills and Enterprise Briefing (May) DfEE, London

Hobsons (2000) *Career Women Casebook 2000*, Hobsons, Cambridge

Pearson, R, Aston, J, Bates, P and Jagger, N (2000) *IES Annual Graduate Review 2000*, Report 367, Institute of Employment Studies, Brighton

Renshaw, R (2000) New role for secretaries, *Interviewer* (January), pp 27–28

Tackey, N and Perryman, S (1999) *Graduates Mean Business*, Report 357, Institute of Employment Studies, Brighton

Times Higher Education Supplement (1999) *First Destinations of UK Domiciled First Degree Holders*, THES, London

Universities and Colleges Admissions Service (2000) *What do Graduates do? 2000: Career Planning for Higher Education and Beyond*, UCAS, Cheltenham

Chapter 2

Handy, C (1989) *The Age of Unreason*, Arrow, London

Sturges, J and Guest, D (2000) *Should I Stay or Should I Go?*, AGR, Warwick

Chapter 3

AGR (2000) *Going to Work on the Web*, AGR, Warwick

Marsh, H (1999) *Nature and Nurture Shape Your First Steps*, Guardian Unlimited, London

Chapter 4

Finney, M (2000) CV-Biodata: its use for CV screening and applicant impression management, *Occupational Psychologist* (August), pp 3–6

Saville and Holdsworth (2000) *The Graduate Challenge*, SHL Group, Thames Ditton

Chapter 5

Income Data Services (IDS) (2000) *Psychological Tests*, IDS Studies Plus: Personnel Policy and Practice, IDS, London

Taylor, S (1998) *Employee Resourcing*, Chartered Institute of Personnel and Development, London

Chapter 6

Clarke, M (2000) All that glitters: incentives on offer for top graduate recruits, *Interviewer* (September), p 18

Institute of Employment Studies (IES) (2000) *Motivating Key People*, IES, Brighton

Sturges, J and Guest, D (2000) *Should I Stay or Should I Go?*, AGR, Warwick

Index

abilities
  application forms   82–84
  communication skills   39–40
  job matching   50–54
  people skills   36–39
  psychometric tests   99–107
  self-organisation   41–43
  thinking skills   43–45
  transferable skills   35–36, 45–46
  types and patterns of   33–35
accountancy   7
achievement   30
  application forms   80–81
  orientation towards   42–43
administrative jobs   2
advertised jobs
  the ideal candidate   67–68
  Internet   60–64
  making sense of adverts   64–68
  newspapers and journals   57–59
application forms
  abilities and skills   82–84
  administrative details   85
  biodata forms   87–89
  declarations   86–87
  employers' and standard   77–78
  etiquette and covering letters   95–97
  explaining career choice   81–82
  interests and achievements   80–81
  on the internet   88
  location preferences   80
  open-ended questions   84–85
  personal details and history   78–80
  referees   85–86
  see also curriculum vitae (CV)
arts and humanities   8–9
  career planning   25–26

assessment centres   121–22
  group exercises   124–25
  other exercises   125–28
  presentation exercises   122–24
  results   128–29
Association of Graduate Careers Advisory
    Services   64
Autumn Graduate Recruitment Fair   71
biodata forms   87–89
Bolles, Richard
  What Color is Your Parachute?   54
Britain's Best Employers   74
Build Your Own Rainbow (Hopson and
    Scally)   54
business and management jobs   7, 9,
    13–14

career planning
  desires and dreams   21–24
  existing interests   24–27
  expectations of a new job   135
  job matching   50–54
  motivations   29–33
  values   28–29
Careers and Occupational Information
    Centre
  Occupations   24
catering   7
clerical and secretarial jobs   7
cold canvassing   73–75
Commission for Racial Equality (CRE)   19
communication   37
  writing skills   39–40
competition   30
computer literacy   40
computer science   7
contracts, employment   130–33

creativity skills   44–45
criminal convictions   85
curriculum vitae (CV)
    electronic and scanned   91, 94–95
    etiquette and covering letters   95–97
    internet recruitment   61, 63
    interview discussion   116, 117, 118
    requirements and presentation   89–91
    sample   92–93
    tailoring to employer   74, 75

design   7
development
    centres   143–44
    fast-track training   2
    for new employees   134–35, 137–40
Development and Assessment Centres
    (Woodruffe)   129
Disability Discrimination Act   85
discrimination
    application forms   85
    employers' biases   14–19
DiversityNow   72
drama   7, 8

EAF (employers' application form)   77–78
economics   7
education
    application forms   79–80
    interview questions   118
    job development   134–35, 137–40
employers
    decoding job adverts   65
    directories of   59
    first impressions   97
    management support   136
    recruitment tactics   57
employment agencies   68–70
engineering   7, 9–10, 17
ethnic minorities   18–19
European opportunities   11–14
executive search   69–70

financial services sector   12–13
flexibility and resilience   42–43

gap year experience   49–50
group work   124–25

Hallet, Heather   17
handwriting   96
head hunters   69–70
health professions   7
Hopson, Barrie
    Build Your Own Rainbow (with Scally)
    54
How to Master Personality Questionnaires
    (Parkinson)   48
How to Master Psychometric Tests   107

How to Succeed at Assessment Centres
    129

industry and manufacturing   13
information technology
    career planning   25–26
    international opportunities   12
    job destinations   7, 10
    see also computer science
interests, personal
    career planning   24–27
    inteviews   119
    job matching   50–53
Internet
    advertised jobs   60–64
    application forms   88
    employer tactics   57
    information for cold canvassing   73–74
    networking   72
    top ten Web sites   62–64
interviews   113–14
    afterwards   120–21
    preparing for   114
    'rule of three' formula   114–20

jobs
    decoding advert descriptions of   66–67
    destinations of graduates   6–11
    market   1, 56–57
    non-traditional for graduates   3
    routes to   2–5
    security   6
jobs, starting
    appraisals and feedback   140–43
    development   134–35, 137–40
    expectations   134–37
    induction   133–34
    staying employed   144–48
judgement   44

Kaleidoscope publications   60
Kelly's directory   73

learning   43
literary occupations   7

Marketing, Retailing and Sales Casebook
    59–60
Marne, Patricia
    Teach Yourself Graphology   96
mathematics   10
mature graduates   16
media   7
medicine   7
mentoring   137–39
milk rounds see recruitment fairs
motivations
    for choosing careers   29–33
    job matching   50–53

National Centre for Work Experience 46
networking 71–72
newspapers and journals
  job advertisement 58–59

Occupations (COIC) 24
100 Best Companies to Work for in the UK 74
organisations
  fitting yourself to 144–48

pay and benefits
  beginning the job 130, 132
  decoding job adverts 64–65
  as motivation 31
  usual offers 5–6
people
  skills 36–39
  working with 25
personality factors
  inteviews 119
  job matching 50–54
  managing the new job 145–46
  psychometric tests 107–09
  types and self-assessment 46–48
  see also abilities
The Personnel Manager's Yearbook 73
power, motivation of 30
presentations 122–24
prestige 31–32
Prince's Youth Business Trust 5
problem-solving 43
professional careers 2, 7
promotion
  expectations 136
  flatter hierarchies 6
  motivation 32
Prospects Directory 60
Prospects Today (journal) 63
psychometric tests 98–99
  abilities 34, 99–107
  administration and interpretation 109–12
  personality questionnaires 107–09

recruitment *see* advertised jobs
recruitment fairs 70–71
referees 85–86
Rehabilitation of Offenders Act 85
relationships 23
reliability 42
retail 7, 11–12
Royal Air Force 103–04

SAF (standard application form) 77–78
salaries *see* pay and benefits

Scally, Mike
  Build Your Own Rainbow (with Hopson) 54
science and technology jobs 7, 10, 17
self-employment 3
  starting out 4–5
self-image
  career planning 23
self-organisation 41–43
self-understanding
  interviews 116–19
Shell LiveWire programme 5
skills *see* abilities
Skills Tracker 46
small firms 3, 75
social sciences 11

Teach Yourself Graphology (Marne) 96
teaching 7
thinking skills 43–45
The Times Higher Education Supplement 11
transferable skills
  interviews 119
  job matching 50–54

United Biscuits 137–39
universities
  employers' biases 14–15
University and Colleges Admissions Service (UCAS)
  What Do Graduates Do? 11

values
  career planning 28–29
  job matching 50–53
veterinary science 7
voluntary sector 75

Web sites *see* Internet
What Color is Your Parachute? (Bolles) 54
What Do Graduates Do? (UCAS) 11
women
  employers' biases 17–18
Woodruffe, Charles
  Development and Assessment Centres 129
work experience 49–50
  application forms 79–80
  CVs 90
  inteviews 119
work-life balance 135–36
work permits 79
writing
  communication skills 39–40